J.A.BALL
MAY '95

D0643724

THE WOODEN ARCHITECTURE OF RUSSIA

HOUSES, FORTIFICATIONS, CHURCHES

THE WOODEN ARCHITECTURE OF RUSSIA

HOUSES, FORTIFICATIONS, CHURCHES

ALEXANDER OPOLOVNIKOV AND YELENA OPOLOVNIKOVA

Edited and introduced by David Buxton

Color photographs by Vadim Gippenreiter

HARRY N. ABRAMS, INC., PUBLISHERS, NEW YORK

Frontispiece Cathedral of the
Transfiguration, Kizhi, Lake Onega. The
upper domes and *bochki* after restoration,
seen from the bell tower

Translated from the Russian by
Julia and Robin Whitby
Maps drawn by Ben Cracknell

Library of Congress Cataloging-in-Publication Data

Opolovnikov, A. V. (Aleksander Viktorovich)
  Wooden architecture of Russia : houses,
fortifications, and churches / Alexander
Opolovnikov and Yelena Opolovnikova : color
photographs by Vadim Gippenreiter : edited
and introduced by David Buxton.
    p. cm.
  Bibliography: p.
  Includes index.
  ISBN 0-8109-1771-8
  1. Building, Wooden—Soviet Union,
Northern.   I. Opolovnikova, E. A. (Elena
Aleksandrovna)   II. Gippenreiter, Vadim
Evgen'evich.   III. Buxton, David Roden, 1910–   .   IV. Title.
NA1181.066 1989
720'.947—dc19   88-25110

Published in 1989 by Harry N. Abrams, Incorporated, New York
All rights reserved. No part of this publication may be reproduced
without the written permission of the publisher

A Times Mirror Company

Printed and bound in Spain
DLTO 2545-1988

Contents

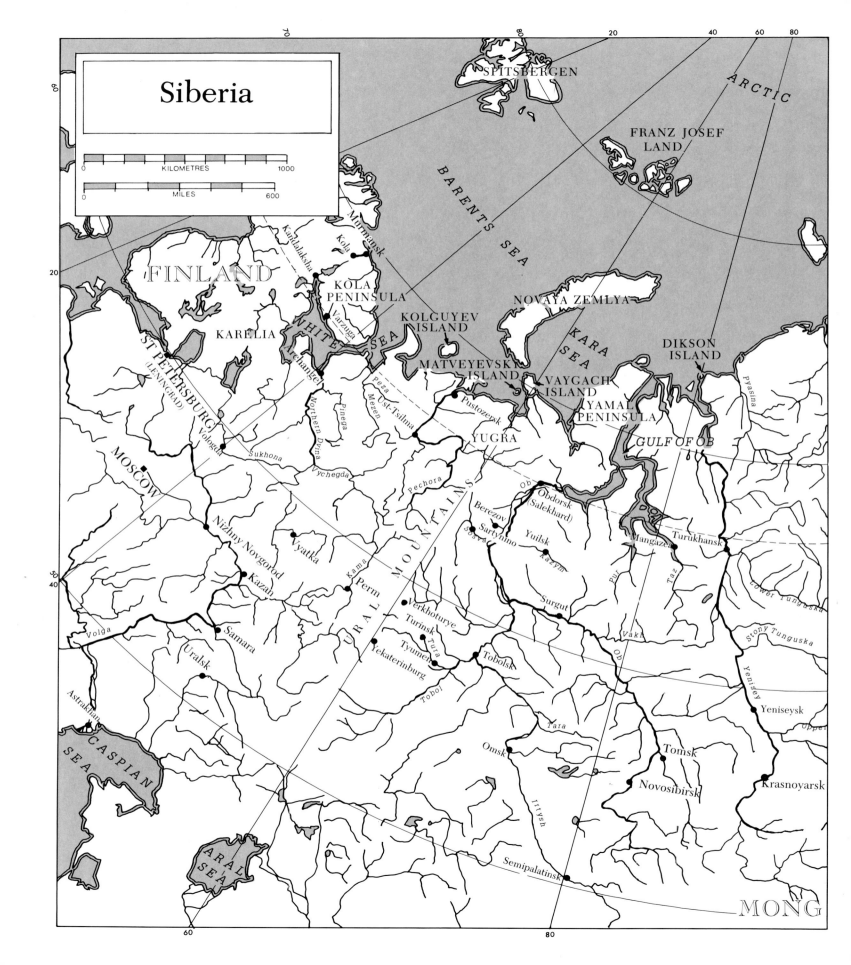

Siberia

KILOMETRES 0 — 1000

MILES 0 — 600

SPITSBERGEN

ARCTIC

FRANZ JOSEF LAND

BARENTS SEA

Murmansk

Kandalaksha

Kola

FINLAND

KOLA PENINSULA

NOVAYA ZEMLYA

Varzuga

KARELIA

WHITE SEA

KOLGUYEV ISLAND

KARA SEA

DIKSON ISLAND

ST PETERSBURG (LENINGRAD)

Archangel

Peza

MATVEYEVSKY ISLAND

VAYGACH ISLAND

Pyasina

Northern Dvina

Pinega

Mezen

Ust-Tsilma

Pustozersk

YUGRA

YAMAL PENINSULA

GULF OF OB

Vologda

Sukhona

Vychegda

MOSCOW

Pechora

Ob

Obdorsk (Salekhard)

Berezov

Turukhansk

Nizhny Novgorod

Vyatka

Sartynino

Sosva

Yuilsk

Mangazeya

Lower Tunguska

Kama

Kazym

Pur

Kazan

Perm

URAL MOUNTAINS

Surgut

Taz

Stony Tunguska

Verkhoturye

Vakh

Ob

Samara

Turinsk

Tura

Yenisey

Uralsk

Tyumen

Tobol

Tobolsk

Upper

Astrakhan

Yekaterinburg

Yeniseysk

Tara

CASPIAN SEA

Irtysh

Omsk

Tomsk

ARAL SEA

Novosibirsk

Krasnoyarsk

Semipalatinsk

MONG

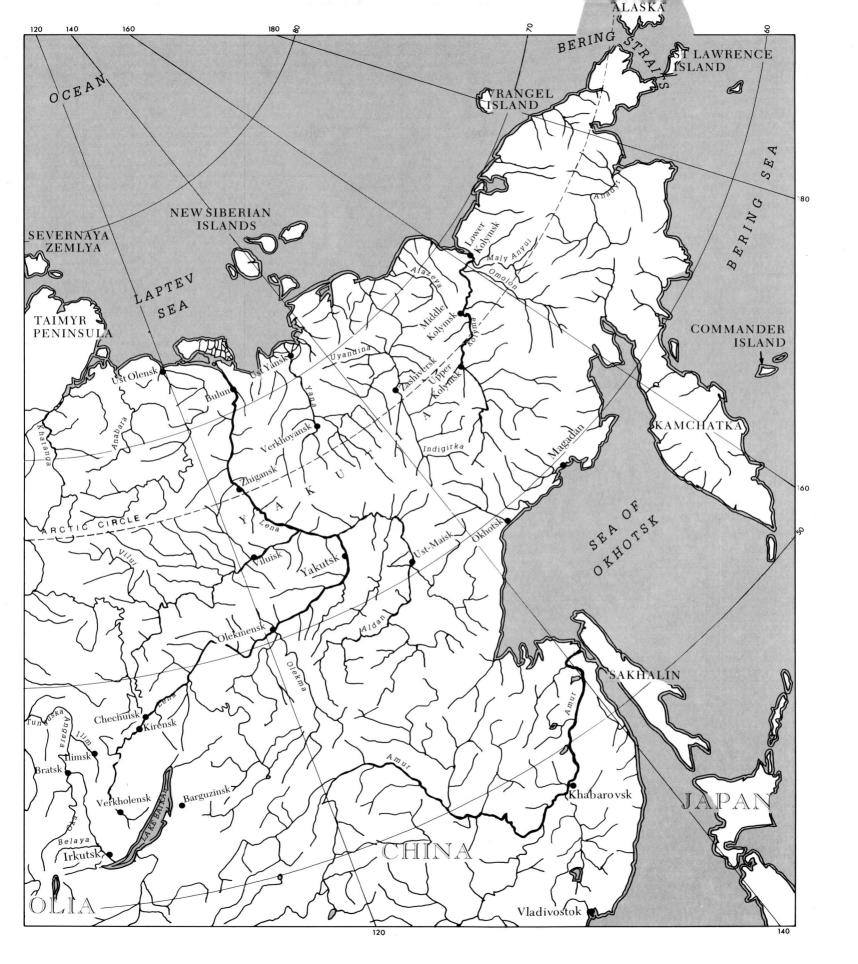

NORWAY

SWEDEN

BARENTS SEA

KOLGUYEV ISLAND

Ob

Kazym

Pustozersk

Berezov

KANIN PENINSULA

Pechora

Kola Murmansk

Ust-Tsilma

URAL

Lyapin

Severnaya Sosva

Irtysh

KOLA PENINSULA

Izhma

Pechora

Umba Varzuga

Mezen

Peza

ARCTIC   CIRCLE

Keret

Azapolye

KOMI A.R.

WHITE SEA

Mezen

Pechora

Archangel

SOLOVETSKY ISLANDS

Lyavlya

Pinege

Kem

Nenoksa

Kholmogory

Pinega

Tura

Turinsk

Suma

Onega

Vazentsi

Northern Dvina

Verkhnyaya Uftyuga

Ustsisolsk (Syktyvkar)

Verkhoturye

Turchasovo

Puchuga

Vaga

Vychegda

Chelmuzhi

Pochozero

Permogorye

Krasnoborsk

Solvichegodsk

Yekaterinburg (Sverdlovsk)

LYCHNY ISLAND

Yandomozero

Vodlozero

Veliky Ustyug

Kama

Perm

Kondopoga

Kizhi

Kargopol

Velsk

Petrozavodsk

LAKE ONEGA

LAKE LACH

Astafyevo

LAKE VOZHE

Sukhona

Vyatka (Kirov)

Chelyabinsk

Olonets

Vytegra

Totma

Kama

Z

Svir

LAKE BELOYE

LAKE LADOGA

Belozersk

Vyatka

Ufa

Helsinki

Neva

ST PETERSBURG (LENINGRAD)

Vologda

Galich

Uren

Belaya

FINLAND

Tallinn

Volkhov

Novgorod

Kostroma

Kineshma

Nizhny Novgorod (Gorky)

Kazan

Belaya

ESTONIA

Yaroslavl

Pless

Ivanovo

Tetyushi

Pskov

Porkhov

Tver (Kalinin)

Rostov Veliky

Pereyaslavl-Zalesky

Suzdal

Vladimir

Simbirsk (Ulyanov)

Samara (Kuybyshev)

Ural

Riga

LATVIA

Volga

Rzhev

MOSCOW

Oka

Orenburg

Veljkie Luki

Kolomna

Zaraysk

Syzran

LITHUANIA

Polotsk

Dvina

Vitebsk

Dnieper

Vyazma

Serpukhov

Ryazan

Shatsk

Penza

Sursk

Uralsk

Kaunas

Kaluga

Vilnius

Minsk

Mogilev

Smolensk

Belev

Tula

Ryazh

Mtsensk

Tambov

Saratov

Bryansk

Oka

Orel

Yelets

Livny

BYELORUSSIA

Gomel

Kursk

Voronezh

Volny

Don

Chernigov

Sumy

Belgorod

Stary Uskol

Tsaritsyn (Volgograd)

Volga

KIEV

Kharkov

Rovno

Poltava

Lugansk (Voroshilovgrad)

Astrakhan

CASPIAN SEA

UKRAINE

Warsaw

POLAND

Brest

Zaporozhye

Rostov-on-Don

European Russia

KILOMETRES

0   500

MILES

0   300

N

Introduction

*J*ust sixty years ago, in the course of youthful wanderings, I spent several weeks in a village called Pokrovo in the region of the upper Volga. It was a traditional village, its way of life as yet little affected by the Revolution. Its fields and pastures were simply clearings in the great forest that covers so much of northern Russia. The forest had yielded the timber for all the dwellings in the village; only the church was of brick. In one of these log-built izbi I was enjoying the hospitality of a peasant family called Pashkov – I had met the father in the market of the small town of Uglich two or three hours' tarantass ride away. The neighbouring forest also yielded an abundance of edible fungi which I joined in gathering – so successfully in fact that I gained quite a reputation in the village. These fungi (Boletus *sp.*) were strung up to dry for the winter.

This then was my introduction to the wooden world of northern Russia which, among the various 'worlds' of Russia (where I had already embarked on an architectural study) was to me the most alluring. Four years later (1932) I was back there, stimulated and immensely helped by Grabar's great History of Russian Art *which is still one of my treasured possessions. Then I journeyed (mostly by steamer but often on foot) through the very regions later beloved of the Opolovnikovs – Lake Onega, the White Sea coasts and that great river, the Northern Dvina. My interests were the same too – churches above all. Those were hard times: I was often very hungry and sometimes found no bed for the night (no wonder I never met another foreigner). But it did not matter. The thrill of the quest amply compensated for any discomforts or trials of travel. So I managed to reach a few of those far-flung villages and to track down at least a sample of their beautiful timber-built churches and belfries.*

During the many years I spent in various African countries as a professional entomologist, and later in the British Council, my interest in eastern Europe and its architecture lay dormant, but I eagerly reverted to it after retirement. It was then that I came across the name of Opolovnikov and realized from his book Restavratsiya Pamyatnikov Narodnogo Zodchestva *(The Restoration of Monuments of Folk Architecture) that he must be a congenial person. Also, a succession of booklets published locally on Kizhi from the 1950s onwards made the importance of his work abundantly clear. As it happened, I had myself become more and more attracted to wooden buildings in particular, not only in northern*

9

Russia but in Ukraine and all the countries that adjoin the Soviet Union to the west. After a number of research trips in those countries during the 1970s I was able to publish my own book on the wooden churches of eastern Europe – a book in some ways complementary to the Opolovnikovs' work.

After the unsympathetic, not to say barbaric treatment of wooden buildings in the nineteenth century (which nevertheless saved some of them from ruin) the early twentieth century saw the emergence of more appreciative and understanding attitudes. Outstanding names of the period known to me from the literature were those of I. Grabar and M. Krasovsky, followed by N. Sobolev and A. Nekrasov, and I once met P. Baranovsky. Outside Russia it was J. Strzygowski, more than anyone, who urged the proper appreciation of wooden churches, pointing out that even quite small ones could have a monumental quality fitting them for serious treatment as monuments of architecture.

In more recent times, in Russia as well as neighbouring states, both specialist and non-specialist writers and photographers have become real devotees of the subject. But I think it is true that in Russia, in this field of scholarship and practical endeavour, Alexander Viktorovich Opolovnikov reigns supreme. He has been the leading force in turning Kizhi Island into one of the world's most fascinating open-air museums, while as architect and master-craftsman he has conducted the restoration of many outstanding wooden buildings there and elsewhere. At the same time he is well aware of the damage that may be done to a village community by removing its finest buildings to a museum site and has concurrently pursued the opposite objective of leaving them, when possible, in their native place. Besides all this, he is obviously sensitive to the spiritual significance of churches, as of icons.

Perhaps the most remarkable thing about this architecture of eastern and northern Europe is that the apparently restrictive principle of building with horizontal logs could lead, especially in churches, to such amazing diversity. This same method of construction produced the log cabins of America, themselves of European origin; but no such fanciful evolution ensued in that part of the world. In Russia it was certainly the far north that witnessed the finest flowering of the style, which may be one reason for the Opolovnikovs' predilection for Karelia, the White Sea and the northern rivers. It might be objected, however, that the rather more southerly provinces of Vladimir, Kostroma, Kalinin, etc., whose wooden buildings are likewise highly evolved, have suffered some neglect. Fortunately the balance is to some extent redressed by Vadim Gippenreiter's admirable colour photographs – an important contribution to the beauty and value of the book.

Outside Europe it is the vast territory of Siberia, which takes Russia right across northern Asia and half way round the world, that has engaged the authors' special interest. No wonder; some of us in Britain have been enthralled by Siberia too. I myself was introduced to the subject long ago by the writings of Henry Seebohm, a Victorian ornithologist and great Siberian traveller. Of course it is the remains of the pioneers' wooden forts, lost elsewhere, that form the basic subject-matter of Chapter 3 in this book, and these are the material witnesses of one of the great epics of history. The penetration of Siberia was dependent, at first, not on any policy of imperialist expansion but on the enterprise and fortitude of individual hunters and traders. Even Yermak's famous campaign (1581–82) against the Siberian Tatars was a private venture: the trading family of Stroganoff employed him, to secure what they regarded as their own territory from intrusion. But in time the state saw potential revenue in the eastward expansion and did become interested. When, later on, we read of Cossack forces among the pioneers it is a sure sign of official involvement.

Exploring ever further eastward by land and water these adventurers discovered the great Siberian rivers (only the lower Ob had been known earlier). Sea voyages to their mouths on the Arctic ocean were attempted and the feasible portages between their various head-streams and tributaries sought out. But in those interminable wastes of swamp and forest winter travel by dog or reindeer-sled was often the only possibility. Winter trails many thousands of kilometres long were gradually established and within some sixty years had extended to the Pacific (1641) and to the remotest regions of the north-east.

What then was the original motive behind these advances into the vast and hostile unknown, at such cost and hazard? Ostensibly the answer is simple: it was the fur trade. But one cannot doubt that the spirit of adventure played its part, and a big one. As to the distant government in Moscow, it was the valuable fur tribute exacted from the Siberian tribes that induced it to support the whole tremendous venture. (Mining came later, as did a very considerable trade in 'fossil' ivory – i.e. mammoth tusks.) Naturally, the tribes did not take such exactions lying down, and the mere existence of all those wooden towers and ramparts proves that resistance was expected. One may be sceptical about the authors' claim that such measures sometimes proved unnecessary, but it seems to be true that the Russian government was much less harsh in its dealings with these indigenous peoples than some colonial powers would have been. In many cases satisfactory relationships were soon established, and a process of mild Russification set in spontaneously. Conversely, the Russian immigrants learnt a great deal from the local tribes, mostly semi-nomadic, about dogs and reindeer, and how to survive in the intense winter cold.

Far beyond Yakutsk, now a modernized city and the metropolis of north-eastern Siberia, lie those ultimate settlements near the Arctic seas which endure the world's severest climate and, at least until the era of air transport, were among the most isolated of all human communities. In the minds of many westerners these inhospitable places are associated with their involuntary residents, some of whom lived to make important contributions to Siberian studies. Then there are zoologists and others who certainly recall the extraordinary story of the frozen Siberian mammoths recovered from the same area, whose flesh was eagerly devoured, after many thousands of years, by wild carnivores and the travellers' sledge-dogs. Neither of these aspects of north-eastern Siberia are mentioned in this book, but we do read of the wooden forts once erected on those remote river-side sites, including the most recent of them all, built on a tributary of the Kolyma in the 1840s.

Much, indeed, can be learnt about the conquest of Siberia from the Opolovnikovs' third chapter. But I wonder if it quite does justice to the immensity of the area or to the human cost of Russia's great eastward expansion. I feel that accounts of travel in the old days help to fill in the picture, for even on well established routes journeys were incredibly long and arduous. Exiled citizens from Moscow, for instance, with their Cossack guards, could spend up to two years on the seemingly endless tramp to the Kolyma settlements. From Yakutsk onwards – the notorious 'Kolymsky trakt' – the trek was reckoned at three months or more.

Yet those privileged to use the very efficient posting system set up under the Tsars could do surprisingly well. This normally meant travelling day and night, changing drivers and horses (or it might be dogs or reindeer) at the posting stations every twenty-four kilometres or so, and snatching what sleep one could while in motion. Thus in November to December 1901, E. W. Pfizenmayer of the Russian Academy of Sciences had to escort eleven sledge-loads of frozen mammoth-carcase from the Kolyma homewards. Generally under reindeer-power he covered the two thousand kilometres to Yakutsk in a month and a half, despite appalling conditions in the two mountain ranges to be crossed (with temperatures down to −55° C) and a stopover in Verkhoyansk. Then in January 1902 he positively raced on to Irkutsk – another two thousand kilometres but much easier going – completing the course in sixteen days and four hours. But he recalled that an English sporting peer, Lord Clifford, had cut five hours off this record by dint of more generous tipping! The last stage of Pfizenmayer's trip, another reminder of the huge distances traversed, was a thirteen-day rail journey from Irkutsk to St Petersburg (but this does sound abnormally long, even for that period).

At this point a word is needed about the American connection with Siberia, even though it falls outside the scope of this book. It was towards the middle of the eighteenth century that Vitus Bering, the great Danish navigator in the Russian service, demonstrated that the Straits which bear his name really divided the eastern extremity of Siberia from the North American continent. This did not discourage the Russians from crossing the intervening seas, pushing on into Alaska, and even establishing a footing in California (then part of the Spanish Pacific empire). The Alaskan adventure was comparatively unsuccessful and short-lived, ending with the sale of the territory in 1867 to the United States. Nevertheless it led to the establishment, at the end of the eighteenth century, of the Russian-American Company, which in effect acted as agent for the Russian government. Then between 1871 and 1917 the Commander Islands off the coast of Kamchatka were leased to American companies trading with eastern Siberia.

If we now revert to the northern marches of European Russia, it is interesting to ask what links with the West are suggested by the Opolovnikovs' text. Surprisingly, there are quite a number, beginning with Richard Chancellor's failed attempt on the North-East Passage in 1553. Many English children have learnt at school how his ship reached Kholmogory on the lower Dvina (later superseded by Archangel), how he travelled thence to Moscow (suffering horribly from the cold), met Tsar Ivan 'the Terrible', and established the first link between Britain and Muscovy. Chancellor is not here mentioned by name, though British interest in a possible Arctic sea-route to China is referred to. We also read that many ships under various flags, including French, Dutch, Swedish and German, frequented the Murman coast and White Sea in the sixteenth century. This suggests that Chancellor's voyage, however important for Britain, was not altogether unusual. Nor, of course, was he the 'discoverer' of Russia, as has sometimes been claimed. A certain Sigismund von Herberstein, Ambassador of the Germanic Empire of those times, had been there earlier in the century and written up his experiences.

In modern times the north-Russian coasts were visited repeatedly by British forces. It is distressing to read, in Chapter 4, of the attack on Kola (near present-day Murmansk on the Arctic coast) in 1854, whereby two wooden churches, many dwellings and some food-stores were burnt, besides the wooden fort. I had to do a little research to find out that this was a side-show of the Crimean War, as was a Franco-British assault on Kamchatka in the Russian Far-East at about the same time. But the authors refrain from mentioning the hostile presence of the British in those northern waters both before and after 1854 (except for a brief reference to the siege of the Solovetsky Islands). In 1810 there had been a similar attack on Kola in retaliation for Russian participation in a continental blockade of Britain. Nearer our own time, in the wretched period of the Russian Civil War, small Allied forces (British, French, Canadian and American) landed at Murmansk and Archangel and even penetrated some way inland. This was all part of the anti-Bolshevik crusade (the Intervention) of 1918–21. Happily the last involvement of our country in those parts – in the Second World War – marked at last an important collaboration in a common cause.

Such are the historic events of which this book, for some people, may be a reminder. However, its subject-matter must be unfamiliar to most readers in Western countries, who will therefore be introduced, for the first time, to an unsuspected world of great fascination and beauty. Alexander Opolovnikov's name is likewise little known outside Russia but he deserves to be honoured as one who has devoted the best part of his life to saving a unique architectural heritage. He did so in a climate of initial indifference which his very labours helped to transform. In conclusion, I should like to extend a warm welcome to Opolovnikov's daughter and co-author, Yelena Alexandrovna, who seems to be following in her father's footsteps.

David Buxton

1 · The Originality of Russian Wooden Architecture

RUSSIAN wooden architecture is a vigorous branch of the national culture, with its roots deep in ancient times. Nearly every artefact of old Russia was made of wood. Men had been settled for centuries by forests bordering rivers and lakes, of which the vast resources provided them with shelter, food and warmth. It was from wood that they built their churches and cathedrals, their houses and cities, with strong walls and fortified towers to protect them. The simple implements of everyday life, from the spoon to the plough, from the cradle to the cross, were all made of wood. Every detail of these objects, however grand or humble they were, was the result of careful thought. Medieval Russian architecture sprang from real life and contained the very essence of the Russians' view of their world, their perception of beauty, indeed everything that goes to make up the character of the nation and its distinctive art. The fruits of such creativity, profoundly national in form and content, make an invaluable contribution to universal human culture, evoking a sense of oneness with nature and with the past.

Wooden architecture, like stone, reflected every important political and economic development in Russian history, as well as the changing philosophical and aesthetic background to Russian life. It was a gigantic research laboratory for architecture as a whole, where new forms and methods could be devised, experimented with, changed and improved. Wooden, stone and brick architecture are related in complex ways, and there was a strong and continuous mutual influence among them. As the art historian Igor Grabar wrote: 'The history of Muscovite architecture is largely the history of wooden design transferred to masonry buildings.'

The origins of Russian wooden architecture lie in the ancient artistic and building traditions of the Kiev *Rus* people, Novgorod the Great and the principalities of Vladimir–Suzdal, but it achieved its finest expression at the time of the gradual establishment of the centralized Moscow *Rus*. The aesthetic and artistic ideals of the time found their most lively and complete embodiment in many extraordinary works, such as the cathedrals of the Moscow Kremlin, the paintings of Andrey Rublev and Dionysus, the Church of the Ascension in Kolomenskoe and the wealth of wooden tent-roof churches. However different these works may be, they all proclaim the ideal of harmony to which the peoples

Drawing of the Chapel of SS Peter and Paul, Volkostrov; north facade (see also plate XXVII)

15

of Russia aspired as they progressed along the path towards independent nationhood.

Wooden churches were being built in Russia from as early as the end of the tenth century, but the surviving examples date from the fifteenth century onwards. The year 980 saw the erection, in oak, of the thirteen-domed St Sophia of Novgorod, a splendid illustration of the great skill and considerable experience of those early architects in the construction of monumental wooden buildings.

Researchers are generally agreed that the earliest wooden churches were based on a quadrilateral framework of interlocking logs (*srub*; the glossary explains the principal terms of wooden architecture). This principle was a limiting factor in the number of possible architectural variations and frequently these churches differed from ordinary dwellings only in having domes and crosses on their gables.

The striving to render churches distinctive, even awe-inspiring, and to give them greater height – an essential ingredient of beauty for the Slavs – led to new architectural solutions which would respect and incorporate the ancient traditions.

The most characteristic product of old wooden architecture is the so-called tent-roof church. There is no documentary evidence as to its exact dates, but it is of great antiquity. The social and philosophical outlook of the Russian people, and the evolution of their own culture, are vividly expressed in tent-roof architecture. The tent shape (*shater*, pronounced *shatyor*) in sacred buildings had its origins in fortification architecture. Wooden watch-towers had been erected in Russia certainly well before the coming of Christianity in the ninth century (Russia accepted Christianity fully only in 988). At first these towers were known as *vezhi*, from the verb *vedat*, to know. Later, from the fourteenth century onwards, when fortified towns surrounded by high wooden walls and towers were being built all over Russia, they were called *strelnitsi*, from the verb *strelat*, to shoot, or *stolbe*, columns. These sombre guardians of the national territory, grimly symbolizing its strength and independence, were a powerful influence on the formation of the aesthetic principles which governed folk architecture.

The typical watch-tower was raised on an octagonal log base, and the simplest and most functional roof for such a structure was an octagonal pyramid, tapering sharply towards the top, and known in Russian architecture as a 'tent'. Watch-towers were usually surmounted by turrets, to improve surveillance of the surrounding country. Churches and bell-towers could be distinguished by their tent-roofs, which were crowned with onion domes placed on small cylindrical drums. Onion domes and drums were dressed with *lemekh* (shingles or carved wooden tiles).

Towers and churches were not always octagonal, however. A considerable number were built on a hexagonal log base, for example the bell-towers in the villages of Sogintsi (near Leningrad) and Philippovskoe (in the province of Archangel), and the remains of the mighty hexagonal tower of Pless in Ivanovo, described by V. V. Suslov at the end of the last century. It is probable that the tent-roof developed from the simple, utilitarian version seen in military architecture to the more elaborate forms found on sacred buildings. In the fifteenth and sixteenth centuries the Russian people were growing more conscious of their national identity. Many hundreds of watch-towers were built during this restless,

11, 12
VII, VIII

152

XXX, 194

XIV

78

95

176, 159

94

dangerous period, when Russia was in a virtually continuous state of war with her neighbours. Church architecture gradually adopted the watch-tower design and especially favoured the octagonal log base with a high pyramidal roof. This tent-roof came to symbolize, not military daring, but the demands of spirituality and the power of the human creative impulse. The architectural heritage of Russia is the product of a tradition of collective experience which transcends individual endeavour. The names of its architects are indeed mostly unknown.

As the centralized Moscow state expanded and strengthened, the increasingly powerful autocracy began to influence the design of great public buildings. The ideal of individual spiritual perfection was supplanted, in the sixteenth and seventeenth centuries, by the glorification of the united Orthodox Russian state and its omnipotent ruler. Orthodox religion played an important role in the life of the state, being used to convey the explicit political message that 'Moscow is the third Rome and there will be no other', and that the grand dukes and tsars of Moscow inherited the traditions of the Roman Caesars. Liberation from the Tatar yoke, the unification of petty princedoms within the Moscow state, the marriage of Grand Duke Ivan III (ruled 1462–1505) to Sophia, the niece of the last Byzantine emperor, Constantine Paleologus, and the conquest of Kazan and Astrakhan, all justified the claims of Moscow to the leadership of Christendom. (In literature, incidentally, such aspirations were expressed in the letters of Filofey, a monk from the Yeleaza monastery in Pskov. Among his correspondents were Grand Duke Vasily III, Myusyur Munekhin, a royal scribe, and Ivan the Terrible himself.) Such new ideas introduced markedly temporal elements into the ritual, structure and appearance of churches. To begin with, the changes were barely noticeable but they gradually increased in importance and eventually blossomed, in the seventeenth century, into a truly secular art.

These changing aesthetic tendencies were greatly stimulated by the advent of a new class of urban craftsmen and merchants, who created their own cultural movements in literature, art and architecture. Earthly life was to be the main subject of the arts; architecture, in particular, became colourful and picturesque. The grim asceticism of the previous era had come to an end.

The major changes in wooden architecture may be traced in the evolution of the tower-like tent-roof church. The proportions became lighter and more elegant, and the lay-out of the church was considerably altered as the *trapeznaya* XXVII, 143 began to assume greater importance. The *trapeznaya* was a meeting-room, but its ancestry goes back to the age when Christianity and paganism co-existed. The original function of the *trapeznaya* as a separate building is illustrated by the Russian word (of Greek origin) *trapeza*, meaning a feast. Pagan feasts survived the advent of Christianity in Russia. They were accompanied by the public drinking of a special beer, consecrated according to pagan ritual. The *trapeznaya* then became the place where the congregation, especially those who had come from afar, might gather and exchange news and opinions with each other before and after the service. Surviving stone churches dating from the tenth to the thirteenth centuries, that is, before the Mongol invasion, have virtually no *trapeznaya*. At that time there were hardly any village churches for the use of the common people; the local nobility built their own near their manor houses and there might have been one, two or even three places of worship, depending on the number of local saints or sacred relics.

As the towns and their populations expanded, so the number of urban churches grew. Every street, every little alley, every 'hundred' formed its own small religious community, called a brotherhood, to build a church in honour of its patron saint. Peasants also formed such brotherhoods but, because of a lack of resources, built chapels rather than churches. The essential rituals of daily life, such as weddings, baptisms and funeral services, were of primary importance to the peasants, and they could be adequately and cheaply performed in the modest country chapels.

These Christian brotherhoods were not subject to the authority of the local nobility; they even appointed their own priests, who could be dismissed if they failed to satisfy the congregation. The brotherhoods also had the right to arbitrate on minor matters, so that a trouble-maker at a local gathering, for example, would be hauled up in front of the elder of the meeting rather than being taken before the regional bench.

The *trapeznaya*, originally the scene of pagan sacrificial rituals, thus became the venue for local meetings and even for courts of law. It was a secular rather than a sacred building and institution. In later times its character was to change drastically as a result of major ecclesiastical reforms.

The secular role was especially marked in the first half of the seventeenth century, in remote provincial villages and towns where, during this 'Time of Troubles' the authority of the state held virtually no sway. The state of anarchy, combined with the brutal Polish occupation, led to the development of a form of self-government (*zemstvo*), mainly in the northern regions of the country. Churches, often the only public buildings in the area, took on a new and completely lay function, becoming the seat of local government. Nearly every church built in the seventeenth century actually incorporated its obligatory *trapeznaya*, and building commissions always contained the formula 'to build a church with a *trapeznaya*'.

189, 191   Adding a *trapeznaya* to a rectangular log building was a relatively simple matter of joining two similar shapes together, but octagonal churches presented complications. In some early churches a rectangular *trapeznaya* was simply added to the west side of the main structure, but this created sharp corners and proved unattractive and inconvenient. A more organic solution, which also enabled a higher and more stable building to be erected, was to construct the *trapeznaya* in the form of a gallery, running round the central octagon on the north, west and south sides (the east side being occupied by the sanctuary). Nearly all the tent-roof churches along the Northern Dvina river were built to this plan; some fine examples are or were to be found in the villages of Lyavlya,

225–28   Belaya Sluda, Vershini, Viya (Viisky) and Panilovo.

A different solution to the problem was to substitute a rectangle for the lower part of the octagonal main building. This is the origin of the design described in official documents of the time and by modern historians, as the 'tent-roofed octagon on a rectangle with a *trapeznaya* attached'. Wooden churches built according to this plan became very popular and widespread throughout northern Russia in the seventeenth and eighteenth centuries. They can be seen in Siberia

234   (in Ilim, for example), in remote Yakutia (at Zashiversk), along the Onega River
201–03, 196   (Yandomozero) and the Northern Dvina (Verkhnyaya Uftyuga, and others), by busy trade routes, on quiet paths in the depths of the taiga, and in towns and

villages throughout the region. The very finest example of this type is the Church
of the Assumption (1774) in the town of Kondopoga, on Lake Onega, not far from
Petrozavodsk.

189

Another notable development was the change from a simple entrance into a
grander, more ceremonial approach. This portal (*kryltso*) incorporated a steep,
wide staircase leading to the church itself on the first floor. This arrangement
made the church much warmer and allowed the ground floor to be used for
secular purposes. Porches had always been an essential and varied artistic
element in wooden architecture, in ordinary dwellings as well as the great houses
of the nobility. The importance of church porches derives from their additional
special function as a platform for public speaking. The tenth-century Cathedral of
St Sophia, for example, had its porch in a prominent position on the south side
overlooking the town square, the meeting point for the democratic assembly
(*veche*) of the Republic of Novgorod the Great. Socio-political awareness was at
its height in seventeenth-century Russia, and the importance of the church for
secular activity is signified by the obligatory *kryltso* and open gallery.

135, 165

A third architectural refinement in seventeenth-century and still more
eighteenth-century wooden churches was the creation of richly elaborate
silhouettes. They were achieved by the use of domes, single or in clusters,
storeyed and *kub* roofs, and gables on different levels. (Domes had been built
since the tenth century, as at St Sophia of Novgorod.) Three outstanding examples
are the cathedrals of the Resurrection in Kola (1684), of the Intercession in
Vytegra (1708) and the Transfiguration in Kizhi (1714).

169
XVII, 157, 158

To quote D. S. Likhachev, an authority on the art and history of Russia: 'This
was a pre-renaissance that never blossomed into a Renaissance . . . because the
city republics of Novgorod and Pskov were suppressed, and the official Orthodox
Church prevailed in its battle with the heretics. The centralized State effectively
destroyed the spiritual life of the nation.' The increased authoritarianism of the
state paralysed ordinary people's freedom of thought and eventually their
capacity to produce a vigorous folk art. The Church thus became the main
instrument by which official attitudes and policies were imposed on the minds of
the masses.

Unification of church and state took place gradually throughout the fifteenth
and the first half of the sixteenth centuries. The Church had not been an
authoritarian institution in feudal Russia; in fact the theocratic tendency only
appeared at the time when the Russian princedoms were being centralized round
Moscow, when it was expressed, in the middle of the seventeenth century, by the
dictum 'spiritual above temporal'.

The centralization of the state necessitated the imposition of a common,
unified church ritual. Christianity had been established in the Kiev *Rus* from
Byzantium in 988, but the passage of time, the vastness of Russia and the divided,
warring principalities had resulted in a great disparity between the various
patriarchates. A seventeenth-century Swedish scholar, Johann Botvid, actually
wrote a book entitled *Are the Muscovites True Christians?* He felt obliged to pose
such a question because the Russian people, while understanding and accepting
Christianity, remained faithful to their ancient pagan and totemic beliefs. The
forms and rituals of religion interested them less than the possibilities it offered
for wisdom, self-knowledge and communion with nature.

The unification of the Church was a painful process. Local clergy generally lived like the peasants themselves, ploughing their fields and earning their bread by the sweat of their brow. They were unwilling to lose the few privileges accruing to them as priests of the brotherhood churches. The monasteries, too, were loath to submit themselves to the central hierarchy of the Church. Well before the introduction of church reform, there were cases of parishioners and priests attacking the envoys of the Orthodox hierarchs, refusing to recognize their jurisdiction and rejecting their blessings with contempt. In 1622 Makary, the Metropolitan of Novgorod, was forced to complain to the Tsar himself that 'archimandrites and priors in monasteries, priests and deacons in churches, and even the ordinary members of congregations do not obey me, Your representative, or my subordinates. They refuse to recognize my legal and canonical authority, and deny me and You, Sire, our rightful tithes.'

These conflicts concerning the organization and ideology of the Russian church in the sixteenth and early seventeenth centuries prepared the ground for the fundamental ecclesiastical reform of 1653–56 carried out by Patriarch Nikon (1605–81), after which local disaffection was transformed into the violent opposition known as the *raskol* or Schism. The *raskolniki* or Old Believers, as they have come to be known in English, lived their lives in deliberate contrast with the slavish and sub-human existence forced on their fellows by the authoritarian state. They rejected physical serfdom – forced labour – as well as spiritual subjection, and formed communities of like-minded people, based on the principle of the common ownership of property as laid down by the Apostles. One of the earliest of these settlements was the Vygovskaya commune, by the White Sea, described by one church historian as a religious community run on communistic principles.

The great stumbling-block of Nikon's reform was the revision of church rituals and sacred books to accord with original Greek sources. The rationale for these revisions was the need to unify the Church under the authority of Moscow, and it was no coincidence that the reform was begun in 1653, on the eve of the extension of Russian sovereignty over the Ukraine the following year.

For poorly educated rural clergy, who relied more on their memory than on their books in their readings of the sacred passages, resistance to new texts may have been more practical than ideological. For the educated clergy, however, the very idea of 'correcting' their sacred books seemed no less than sacrilege.

Shortly before Nikon's appointment as Patriarch of Moscow, the Patriarchate had published the *Book of Faith* in which the Greek Church was portrayed as 'adulterated' and as having lost its pure orthodoxy under the influence of the 'Turkish Mohammed' and the Roman Catholic Church. The example *par excellence* of this degeneration was its adherents' iniquitous manner of making the sign of the cross using two fingers, instead of the correct Orthodox method using three.

Nikon first enraged his opponents among the Old Believers with his revision of all the Russian Orthodox holy books by reference to the Greek sources so recently condemned in the *Book of Faith* and then compounded his offence by using Greek texts published in Paris and Venice. The Archpriest of the Kazan Cathedral in Moscow, Ivan Neronov, reproached Nikon: 'You praise the canons of foreigners and accept their traditions. You call them the pious spiritual fathers of our true faith. And yet you yourself have often declared in the past that those same Greeks and [Uniate] Little Russians have abandoned the true faith and steadfastness of spirit, that they have lost their morality . . .'

Old Believers, defending their perception of true Orthodoxy, were joined in their opposition to the reform by the common people, whose freedom had been curtailed by the Russian Law Code of 1649. They found support, too, from many members of the nobility hostile to the autocratic policies of Alexey Mikhailovich, Tsar of Moscow and all the Russias (the father of Peter the Great).

Nearly all strata of the population had begun to participate in political life through the medium of local government which sprang up in the 1550s. Even state-owned serfs took part in the 1613 'Assembly of the Land', which is famous for having elected Tsar Mikhail, the founder of the Romanov dynasty. But by the end of the seventeenth century local government had lost virtually all its power. The Assembly met ten times under that same Mikhail Fedorovich; under his son, Alexey Mikhailovich, it met not once in all the second half of the century. During this period the *Duma* (council) of the Boyar nobility also diminished in importance. Similarly, the army of clerical and temporal officials was placed under strict supervision and later controlled by a special body, the Office of Secret Affairs (*Prikaz tainnikh dyel*), a sort of Privy Council. It was presided over by a commoner and scribe, Dementy Bashmakov. Archpriest Abbakum, the leader of the Old Believers and the most passionate opponent of Patriarch Nikon, called Bashmakov 'the secret agent of the Antichrist'.

Ecclesiastical changes, together with the increase in state power, resulted in a mass migration of people opposed to these developments. The Old Believers fled to the north and to Siberia, out of reach of the Patriarch's authority, where they zealously followed the old traditions, piously preserving them in their daily life as well as in their art and architecture. They reasserted the rights, lost as a result of the reforms, to unfettered movement, to ownership of the land they worked and to self-government. They genuinely could not understand or accept the new Law Code and other administrative measures aimed at preserving order in the state, and they rejected the forcible subordination of the spirit to *raisons d'état*. The Old Believers and their followers now felt themselves to be oppressed from two sides: economically enslaved by the landowners and deprived of their spiritual freedom. Thus began the process of the dehumanization of the Russian peasant: a good Christian, he was stripped of the most fundamental of all human rights, the right to his own beliefs and ideas.

Other classes were also hostile to the increasing bureaucracy in social life and the new legal system, which they found too rigid and formal. People were asked to abandon their traditional sense of right and wrong, the wisdom of generations, and to replace it with the unquestioning obedience demanded by the autocracy. The results were tragic: this blind, enforced subordination stripped men and women of their self-awareness and human dignity, and forced their natural instincts and energies into distorted and extreme forms in an attempt to evade the existing laws. A powerful ideological movement opposed to the official Church, and compromising many different social groups, had been forged around 1640. Yermolai Erasmsky headed the peasants; Feodosiy Kosoy was prominent among leaders of the new urban classes; Fedor Karpov, Ivan Peresvetov and Maxim Grek were the principal representatives of the anti-establishment nobility.

Kosoy, for example, wrote that 'we are all the children of God, capable of knowledge and self-knowledge, for we all have minds and are all spiritual brothers in the truth.' He proclaimed the ideals of brotherly love and equality among all nations.

The persecution of the Old Believers, who had fled to the remote corners of the country from the 'kingdom of the Antichrist', began immediately after the reform at the end of the 1650s. At first it was directed against individuals, but in 1684 a decree was promulgated ordering the suppression of entire settlements: 'Arrest all criminals and Old Believers, destroy their homes, burn down their fortresses, put their ring-leaders in chains and send them to Moscow.' Old Believers desperately defied their tormentors, frequently choosing to die by fire in mass suicides; by the end of the seventeenth century the number of suicides had reached nine thousand, a huge proportion of the population at that time.

The Old Believers never doubted the justice and inevitable victory of their cause. A. Lopukhin, sent to one rebellious region at the head of a police detachment, reported to the Tsar in Moscow: 'Many of them, Sire, do not eat for a week or more. They refuse to speak and reject our priests and icons.' Archpriest Abbakum explained the reasons for resistance in his sermons: 'You suddenly changed our holy rites and all the laws of our church! How could my beloved fellow Christians not be heartbroken? My poor people toil six long days and when on the Sabbath, they come to their church to pray to God and ask a blessing on their labours – why, there is nothing godly for them to listen to: the service is sung in Latin, by damned pagans! What else can poor Christians do but hurl themselves into the flames? They will all burn, in the name of Jesus Christ, before they obey you, you dogs! And every good Christian should follow where they lead. It will be to our eternal glory that we perish in the fire, in the name of our Lord and of the holy fathers and our reward will be life everlasting.'

Abbakum was a passionate egalitarian: 'God created us all equal and we are all entitled to an equal share of His gifts. . . . Heaven and earth belong to us all, bread and water should be shared by all.' He even addressed God as an equal, seeing him as a defender of the people's rights. He spoke of his sworn enemy, Patriarch Nikon, with pure hatred: 'With God's help, I'll smash your snout in for you, well before the Day of Judgment! . . . You son-of-a-bitch, you hound, you threw our country into chaos! I'll gouge your eyes out, I'll throw you out on your neck! Begone into outer darkness! You are not fit to stand in the light of the Lord!'

In the middle years of the seventeenth century it was the urban population that made up the main opposition of Old Believers to the reforms. Some ten or twenty years later they were joined by the nobility and towards the end of the seventeenth century the peasants began to outnumber all the rest. By this time the movement was at its height, but internal divisions soon led to weakness and decline in the eighteenth century.

The Church itself finally lost its independence in the first quarter of the eighteenth century, when it was reduced to a mere department of the state apparatus. It was known as the Holy Synod and supervised by a Chief Procurator. In the nineteenth century the term 'church' was no longer used in official documents and was, instead, referred to as the 'Department of the Orthodox Faith'. 'The eparchy [diocese] of the righteous had become an eparchy of bureaucrats in cassocks', as Nikolai Leskov, the nineteenth-century author, bitterly observed. Even P. V. Verkhovsky, a pious historian of the Holy Synod, was forced to admit: 'The Muslim hegemony over the eastern Orthodox world from 1453 [the fall of Constantinople] enslaved the Orthodox Church and its faith less effectively than Synodic rule in Russia itself.'

We have described the history of the Russian Schism in such detail because it was the Old Believers who defended and preserved the traditional way of life, the art and above all the churches of medieval Russia. They were the only effective resistance to the formidably overwhelming power of the state.

The Patriarch's decision to reimpose the Byzantine canons of worship led to a ban on the tent-roof churches beloved of Old Believers: from then on only the church with five domes, the symbol of true Orthodoxy (in official eyes), was to be allowed. The *trapeznaya* lost its role as a public meeting place and became an extension to the main building. It was used for religious services, becoming larger and more grandly decorated. Old Believers, however, especially the refugees in remote areas who had held onto their independence, persisted in building in the old way. Sometimes they were obliged to compromise; an example of such an 205 accommodation with the authorities may be seen in the Onega village of Vazentsy, where a tent-roof co-exists with the obligatory five domes.

The new churches, with their multi-domed, *kub*-shaped or tiered roofs, never enjoyed great popularity; the approved, heavy 'Russian-Byzantine' style was no more than a short-lived fashion. Nevertheless, the church reforms of the seventeenth century and its subsequent bureaucracy had a direct and most deleterious effect on sacred architecture. In the words of Gogol: 'They are gone, those days, when burning faith directed every mind and thought and deed towards a single end, when churches strove to reach the heavens, their glorious spires soaring above our earthly dwellings as our eternal souls above our mortal flesh.'

The unremitting programme of persecution undertaken by the state and the Synod led to the final suppression of the Old Believer movement by the middle of the nineteenth century. A veritable 'crusade' was instigated against their churches, chapels and monasteries under the pretext that they had become too dilapidated and dangerous to be allowed to stand. The sad decline of the Daniilovsky Monastery, for instance, one of the proudest symbols of the Schism, dates from 1841. The process was begun gradually but deliberately in that year, when a hundred peasants were billeted by the authorities on land belonging to the monastery. The Old Believers were gradually evicted and the prosperity of the community was undermined. The final blow was the destruction of the buildings themselves, including the cemetery, in 1864.

This community, also known as the Vygoretsky Monastery, was situated on the river Vyg, in the northern Onega district. The headquarters of the whole Old Believers movement and its most sacred site, it was also one of the largest and most important economic and cultural centres of northern Russia. It had several grain wharves, two saw mills, many windmills and several tanneries. The monastery minted roubles (which, being of pure silver, were more valuable than those of the state) and provided the entire northern region with icons and religious books. D. V. Filosofov, a well-known art historian and a colleague of Alexandre Benois and Leon Bakst, wrote sadly: 'Daniilovsky was a university as well as a centre for the spread of education among the peasants. Now it has all vanished as though it had never been. This pogrom was just one small episode in our history, but what a lesson it taught us! It is a perfect symbol of the attitude of the authorities to Russian culture. And what did they get out of it? Nothing but ignorance and loss of faith.'

The demise of the Old Believers' movement spelt the end of wooden church construction. The mass building of brick churches now got into its stride. Those wooden churches that had survived were vulgarly and insensitively 'restored'

168, 169   beyond recognition. Their silhouettes and decoration, which the official hierarchy pronounced crude and debased, were prettified according to the eclectic fashion of the day, or else encased in plain boarding inside and out. Their austere rectangular windows were replaced by italianate semi-circular affairs; insubstantial double doors with glass panels were substituted for the massive originals which had been carved out of one huge block of wood. The intricate shingle roofs were hidden by metal sheeting or dull and inappropriate nailed timbers. The proportions of the modest belfries were distorted by clumsy balustrades. Classical porticos, pilasters and arches were added; though elegant in themselves, they were completely alien. And the boxed-in porches and galleries stuck out from the exteriors like ugly crates.

Interiors also suffered drastic changes. The wall dividing the church proper

141, 142   from the *trapeznaya* disappeared, and the decoratively carved supporting posts were totally obscured by timber casing. The newly boxed walls were papered, plastered or painted. Gilt frames, mass-produced in urban factories, replaced the original iconostases. The finely ornamented wooden ceilings were clothed in gaudy canvas or repainted in garish colours; even worse, they were sometimes overpainted with dark blue oil paint and 'decorated' with stars of plywood and gilt.

Just when this desecration was at its height, however, a new respect for the national heritage and traditional culture arose among the progressive and democratic intelligentsia of the country, especially after the abolition of serfdom and the limited political reforms of 1861. This new interest stimulated a search for authentic Russian themes and elements in literature, theatre, music, art and architecture. Expeditions were organized to scour the remote regions of northern Russia and Siberia for ancient churches, chapels and monasteries that had

4   survived, but these people became equally interested in the ordinary dwellings of

X, 46, 52, 71   peasants, their windmills, bridges, wells and barns. The majority of these buildings were entirely made of wood. The scientific study of the cultural past had begun and with it the resistance to official vandalism. One of the most passionate campaigners for the preservation of the national architectural heritage was L. V. Dal, who in 1874 condemned the ecclesiastical authorities for 'rewarding the restoration and destruction of our ancient sacred buildings with equal generosity'. Other experts who mourned the passing of these ancestral glories were V. V. Suslov and F. E. Buslayev; the art historians and architects V. D. Mileyev, P. Pokrishkin, A. A. Karetnikov, I. Grabar, F. Gornostayev and K Romanov; and the painters Ivan Bilibin, Vasily Vereshchagin, N. Shabunin and V. Plotnikov.

The Archaeological Commission was set up at the end of the nineteenth century. It greatly contributed to the protection of ancient wooden buildings from the depredations of officialdom as well as from the ravages of time and the elements. Among its successes are churches in the villages of Yandomozero,

Tsyvozero, Puchuga, Zachatye, Verkhovye, Chelmuzhi, Panilovo and Belaya Sluda (the last two unfortunately burnt down in the 1920s and 1960s respectively). These churches were all carefully renovated and rebuilt according to the strictest principles under the supervision of Mileyev and Karetnikov, the founders of the modern method of restoring ancient monuments in the USSR.

This method, now developed and improved, is being applied to the preservation of those wooden architectural monuments still in their original surroundings, as well as others in numerous open-air museums. A remarkable example of such work is the completely authentic restoration in the 1950s of the entire architectural complex on Kizhi Island in Lake Onega. It includes the world-famous twenty-two-domed Cathedral of the Transfiguration, the ten-domed Church of the Intercession, its bell-tower and the fence with its elaborate turreted gates. This project, the first of its kind undertaken in the Soviet Union, was executed under the supervision of the present author. It was followed by restorations of the Cathedrals of the Assumption in Kondopoga and Kem, the church of St Barbara in Yandomozero and many others.

Russian wooden architecture has much to offer us in the twentieth century. Its majestic simplicity reflects the spiritual strength of the nation which created it. It speaks to us of the lost beauty of our lives and of the creative power of goodness and truth.

1   Detail of a carved spinning-wheel

2 · Domestic and Agricultural Buildings

Life has thrown new
Beams of light on my star
Yet I still sing the hue
Of my golden izba.

THUS wrote Sergey Yesenin, that most Russian of poets, bidding farewell to his early life with a mixture of sadness and joy. Change implies loss: some break with the past. This is in the natural order of things and, like joy and sadness themselves, an inseparable part of the human condition. Nature has always provided shelter for man. The Russian *izba* (basically a log-built dwelling) and the village (also constructed almost entirely of wood) were a continuation of the natural world, fashioned and transfigured by man, to be sure, but always preserving its primal essence: the tree lived on in the logs, the timber floors and ceilings, the polished tables and benches. The Russian peasants' *izba* was more than their home: it was their entire world, reflecting the universe and their place therein. Their house served as fortress and refuge. Its ornament and detail symbolized all that they needed and asked for from nature; it expressed, too, their oneness with it. 'A horse [that is, an ornament on the gable] on the roof brings peace to the home' goes an old saying.

Wood utterly dominated the northern *izba*. Nearly everything was made by the peasants themselves. Hardly anything was bought, for money was scarce. People spent the long winter evenings carving spoons, bowls and toys for the children; they fashioned baskets of birch bark for berries, honey, mushrooms and salt. The women were particularly proud of their spinning-wheels and competed fiercely to show off the finest carved and painted examples, of which it is hard to find two identical specimens. The looms were also made of wood but they were simple, utilitarian objects and evidently not for show.

The walls and the roof of the *izba* offered the peasants some defence against the elements but more importantly they enclosed their particular corner of the universe, illuminated by the sun and protected from the dark forces of evil. The sun symbolized the protective powers, and was usually depicted in three positions on the roof of the *izba*. At dawn and dusk they were on the *prichelini*.

III, IV
1

I

27

2   Example of a *polotentse* from a house at Kuznetsy, Karelia. Its position can be seen in 4

3   Carved extremity, with the date 1880, of a *prichelina*, also from Kuznetsy

4   Kholm, Archangel Province. The ridge-beam or *shelom* of this house terminates in an imaginary creature. A *polotentse* hangs from the summit of the gable, from which point carved *prichelini* also descend. Two *vypuski* (consoles) which help to support the eaves are visible

5   The heraldic beast of Kholm

6–7 (*above, left and right*) Simple traditional *izba* at Maliye Khalui, Archangel Province. The main supports of the roof (*slegi*) are seen projecting under the eaves at the gable-end. Other complications of the roof as in 35 are wanting

8 (*left*) Vorobyi, a hamlet among the Lake Onega islands, Karelia

9 (*above*) Volkostrov, another typical village on an island north of Kizhi. See also 42–3 and plates XXVII, XXVIII

10 Varzuga. A village on the Kola Peninsula near the White Sea, and very close to the Arctic Circle. Its notable wooden church is shown in detail elsewhere (210–11 and plates XXXI, XXXII)

2 *Prichelini* were ornamental timbers on the gables concealing the log-ends. At noon the sun was on the *polotentse* (a shorter, vertical board hanging from the apex of the gable). Carved *polotentsa* with symbolic suns cut into them represented the purity of human intentions, inextricably interwoven with the sunlit rapture of life itself and the victory of light over darkness.

The same symbolic idea of enlightenment and illumination is expressed inside the dwelling in the so-called *krasny ugol* (literally, beautiful corner). It was in this corner that the icons were to be found; its ceiling symbolized the vault of heaven, and the white supporting beams, the Milky Way. Ancient folk wisdom maintained that everything had its purpose: peasants sought and found mythic allies all around them in the forests, fields and rivers. Men were not nature's conqueror, and they should try, not to pit themselves against it, but rather to live in peace with it, while vigorously using and intensively husbanding its treasures. The forest nourished the peasants but they wrested from it meadows for pasture and land for cultivation. Every tree they cut down was used for a specific purpose; nothing was wasted.

8–10 When the traveller comes upon a northern village the first impression is of a higgledy-piggledy collection of dwellings, store-houses, barns, sheds and fences. Closer examination of this apparent disorder reveals a strict regularity, simplicity and rational exploitation of every inch of usable land, land won from an implacable environment. Every building blends into the surrounding landscape extraordinarily well, becoming an organic extension of nature adapted to human needs. This is the essence of the northern village: the beauty of the earth married to the beauty of human creativity.

Nearly every hamlet is an example of this 'planless' building. Bigger villages, bowing to the dictatorship of official planning authorities, have all but lost their original contours and only rarely reveal traces of 'unplanned' building, together with other relics of the past such as the *kurnaya izba* (a house with a stove but no real chimney), windmills, crosses at village boundaries and so on.

Every building in the traditional northern village has its own particular appearance and silhouette, but one common feature unites them: the method of their construction, that of interlocking logs, is a powerful, flowing medium for the diurnal play of light and shade, reflecting every nuance of the natural wood.

Rural builders in southern parts of Russia readily perceived beauty in simple, undecorated walls built of natural stone. Similarly, northern village builders appreciated the natural grace inherent in the basic log framework which was carefully, lovingly worked in accordance with the highest technical and aesthetic standards. The log structure (*srub*) not only served as the functional, practical foundation of each building; it also contained all the artistic and expressive elements common to these villages.

There was a general relationship between the length of a log and its thickness, and its size limited and defined the uses to which it could be put. This, in turn, contributed in no small measure to the organic unity of all the buildings in a group. Logs tended to be grouped in sizes, and logs in any one building would be of the same size. This sameness, repeated several times, took on the character of an architectural module superimposed on buildings of very varied design.

Obviously, this applies equally to the wooden roof tiles, to the *prichelini* and to the *shelomi* or *okhlyupen* (hollowed-out logs running along the ridge of the roof).

COLOUR PLATES

I Detail of the facade of a 19th-century house in Suzdal (compare *prichelina* and *nalichnik* in glossary)

II An unusually elaborate *nalichnik* on a house in Gorka, Archangel Province

III Carved wooden shovel for gathering berries, from Karelia

IV Ceramic pottery, broken then repaired with birch bark, Kizhi, Lake Onega

V Yakovlev house and its barn (*left*); 19th century. Now at Kizhi

VI Yelizarov house, from Medvezhegorsky ('bear mountain') District, Karelia; 19th century. Re-erected at Kizhi

II

III

IV

V

VII

VIII

This is so for all those other parts of the building whose sizes were either identical to the 'log module' or else directly or indirectly derived from it. That is why these village buildings give the impression of being related, of having been built by one architect at one time. The same integrity of style which united the settlements applied to the interiors as well. Did this unity arise from the deliberate acts of individual village carpenters, or from the unself-conscious efforts of many generations? One thing is certain; those people were sharply aware of their oneness with the environment. They created their settlements as well as their individual buildings in accordance with the canons of natural beauty.

There are a number of features common to all ancient Russian wooden architecture which give it great homogeneity. Tradition imposed the same character, texture and style on the buildings, however different their function, shape and size, to create a perfect architectural ensemble in harmonious counterpoint to the natural environment. It would, of course, be wrong to compare these modest hamlets with world-famous architectural masterpieces. Our task is simply to discover the basic creative methods of the early architects.

POCHOZERO

The smallest administrative division in tsarist Russia was the *volost*. Nearly every *volost*, or at least its central section, consisting of a substantial village, is an architectural and compositional unit, held together by common materials, building traditions and landscape.

At first sight the village seems to have been created from one piece of wood by one craftsman. The typical design consists of a nucleus and additional elements. One such is the *okolitsa* (gate) in the *oseki* or *priaslo* (stockade) round the village. This is the beginning and the end of the village: the *okolitsa* greets you as you arrive and bids you farewell as you leave. The stockade is the flank of the ensemble; the nucleus itself has a centre: a votive cross, a chapel, church or some dominant natural feature such as a group of trees or a high river-bank.

To illustrate the *volost's* unity, let us take as an example a remote area of Archangel Province. A narrow forest road leads from Kargopol to Yangary and Kazhozero, passing through a few other *volosti* – Pershlakhta, Pochozero, Kuzminskaya. Between them, many dozens of miles of thick conifer forest and nothing else, apart from a bench, traditional in this area, for tired travellers to rest their weary limbs while they gaze at the panoramic view, the shimmering lake behind the trees, the limitless blue, all the way to the White Sea. Another few miles and there are farm fences along the road, and other signs that a settlement is near: groves of alder and birch, meadows and haystacks. Now the young forest thins out, giving way to green fields and there is a simple and graceful chapel on a hill just to the right of the road. Its porch and gallery face the village, but the first view is of the main facade. To one side is a long log-built bridge, and on the far bank of a little stream a tiny hamlet of just two households. A vast panorama surrounds it. Fields and villages are scattered along the roads and the hilly banks of the lake; and at the very heart of the whole settlement is the *pogost* of Pochozero. (Originally the *pogost* was an administrative division and its centre;

41

11 The commonest type of intersection (*v oblo*) at the corners of wooden buildings in northern Russia. The ends of the timbers project (compare plates VII, VIII)

12 Interior view of a similar intersection: the timbers are smoothed down

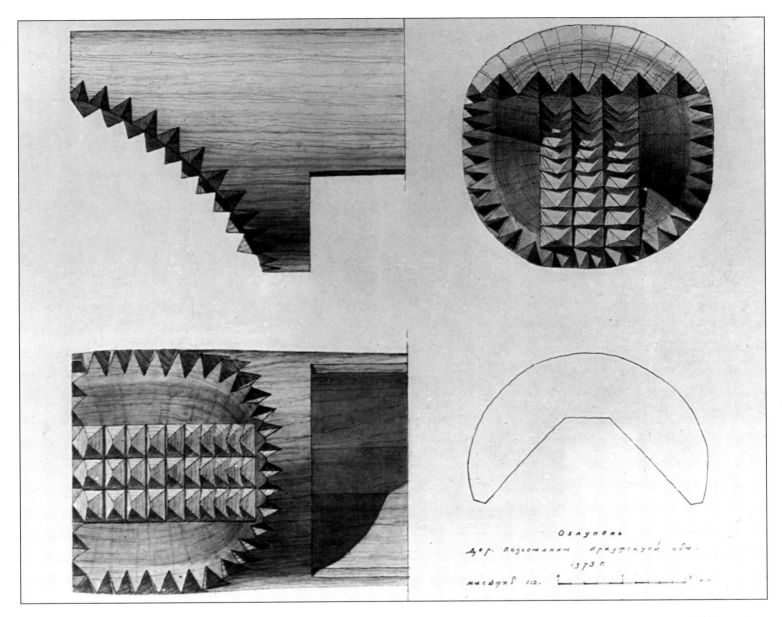

13 Detail of the hollowed-out beam (*shelom* or *okhlyupen*) from a house at Podyelanka, Irkutsk Province, Siberia. Above: side view of decorative projection at the gable-end and end-on appearance of the same. Below: the projection as seen from below and transverse section of the main beam

14   Supports for the drying of hay (*veshala*) in Karelia

15   An alternative system for hay-drying, Archangel Province

later it meant a church with its cemetery and associated clerical dwellings; *see* Chapter IV).

The *pogost* of Pochozero consists of a summer and a winter church, and a separate tent-roofed (*shater*) bell-tower, all enclosed by a fence. It is one of the outstanding monuments of old Russian wooden architecture for domestic and agricultural buildings. The special feature of this *pogost* is that the bell-tower and both the churches are ranged in an almost straight line, at right angles to the road, allowing the traveller the best possible view. In the centre of the village, just by the churches, there is an irregular square with alleys leading off it. In the forest itself, in the shade of ancient firs and pines, there is a long wooden fence round the cemetery, with its modest lych-gate. Further on can be seen a tiny, simple chapel and, by its side, an enormous carved memorial cross, typical of the region.

Every building, every detail and feature of the landscape takes on artistic and emotional significance in the relationship between architecture and nature. The ancient northern dialect word for a fork in the road is *rostan*, equivalent to 'parting'. Such a detail may seem out of place in an architectural study but the resonance of this word, still used today in northern Russia, evokes memories, of farewells and of reunion. At the *rostan* people say goodbye to their loved ones. There is often a sturdy bench at the *rostan*, a mute witness to those last moments.

On the outskirts of the village stands an intriguing construction: a few high posts, placed in a row at four or five-yard intervals, with several long, thin poles fixed horizontally between them. This is the *veshala* for drying hay. Nowadays this characteristic feature of the old northern landscape, like so much else connected with traditional farming methods, has all but disappeared. Occasionally a temporary, jerry-built *veshala* can be found, only strong enough to last for one season. The traditional one, however, was solid, carefully constructed and decorated with carvings.

The Archangel district has another traditional method for drying hay. Young fir trees, stripped of their bark, were placed in a row. The branches were cut off, but their stumps were left and used as natural hooks for the hay to hang on.

HOUSES

Such architectural monuments are part of the folk-memory. The northern *izbi* tell us how people lived in the era of Novgorod the Great and the Moscow *Rus*. There was plenty of land, timber and labour. The buildings were spacious (up to 3000 cubic metres), solid and comfortable, one or two storeys high, with an attic and a covered yard. The homestead was made up of two separate entities, domestic and agricultural. The relationship between them varied from region to region. Thus in southern Russia and in Siberia the farm buildings were placed away from the domestic quarters round an open courtyard separated from the road by a high, solid fence. In northern Russia, by contrast, only store-houses, barns and threshing-floors were built away from the main house; all other buildings – stables, cattle-sheds, haylofts, sometimes even wells – were incorporated into the large, main house under a common roof. Such an arrangement was presumably dictated by the harsh conditions in which the peasants pursued their subsistence economy: they had to reckon with very long, cold winters and enormous amounts of snow; their communities were isolated from each other, with such roads as there were impassable in spring and autumn. Thus, people could go about their work without leaving their house. This type of homestead formed one of the traditions of Russian wooden architecture.

Peasant homesteads are also the architectural embodiment of the close patriarchal system. Fathers and children, sons and grandsons lived under one roof as a single, large family. Land, livestock and farming equipment were all held in common. The head of the family was typically the oldest member of the clan, usually the father of married sons with their own families. These families made up one household but each occupied a separate *izba*. Such a household could provide up to twenty-five pairs of hands to work in the fields. It might consist of four or six *izbi* for accommodation, in addition to the various farm buildings.

The *izbi* were of various types. One of them went by the name of *brus*, literally an oblong beam. In the *brus*, domestic and farm buildings were ranged in one row under a single, double-sloping, gabled roof. A roomy entrance hall with a porch divided this row into two unequal parts: the shorter, containing the living quarters, faced the road and formed the main facade. The larger portion, to the rear, consisted of a covered yard and included other farm buildings. Of course such *brus* houses were not all identical: there were many internal and external variations. Some were simple and functional; others were architectural masterpieces.

Another kind of household was the *glagol*. In the old Russian alphabet *glagol* was the word for 'G', which was written like an inverted Roman capital 'L'. In the *glagol* the farm buildings were placed at right angles to the living quarters.

Yet another variation was the *koshel*, where all the domestic and farm buildings formed a square under a common, massive gabled roof. But the two sides of the roof sloped at different angles, producing an asymmetrical effect. One slope, over the living quarters, was steep and short, while the other, over the farm buildings, was long and gentle, recalling the shape of the traditional *koshel* – a bag or basket.

The appearance of the northern village changed as time went by. Old houses gradually disappeared, many of them being transferred to open-air museums, such as that at Kizhi on Lake Onega. The Onega district was an ancient dependency of Novgorod the Great, whose inhabitants brought to the region the free spirit of that great medieval republic and, in effect, began the tradition of old Russian wooden architecture. The Novgorodians began to settle in the area, hitherto virtually deserted, as early as the eleventh century. Within a hundred years it was already quite densely populated and by the end of the fifteenth century the whole area, including Novgorod itself, had become part of the unified Russian state with Moscow as its capital.

Peasants made up the entire population. They worked hard on their new land and felled whole forests to make way for fields and settlements. They were toughened by their struggle with the cruel elements and never grovelled before exploiters, Russian or foreign. The blight of serfdom hardly affected these northern parts of Russia. Peasants remained relatively free, only paying a land-tax directly to the state. It was thus attractive to Old Believers and many settled here in the latter part of the seventeenth century, to escape Nikon's reforms.

23

16   Pochozero, a village lying to the west of the River Onega (not the great lake of the same name) in the vast Archangel Province. Visible are a fine two-storeyed *izba* and a 'tented' church

17–18   The cemetery or *pogost* of Pochozero. Internal and external views of its formidable log-wall which resembles a defensive rampart

19–20   The Pochozero *pogost*. Two entrances, the 'lych-gate' (above) being capped by a small 'tent-roof'

21–2 Buildings of a country estate at Podyelanka on the River Angara, Irkutsk Province, Siberia. Restored front and side elevations (above) and corresponding sections (below)

The era of Peter the Great (1682–1725) brought change to Onega. New ironworks were built at the time of the Northern War between Russia and Sweden (1700–21). Villages expanded and one new town, Petrozavodsk, was founded. In subsequent decades, however, Onega found itself isolated from the mainstream of Russian history. Local peasant life retained its traditions and customs in all their original purity. Gradually the area became a treasury of ancient Russian culture: local icons preserved the finest traditions of medieval Novgorod painting long after they had been forgotten in other northern provinces. The famous Vladimir *bylini* (Russian traditional heroic poems) had their origin in the Kiev *Rus* but survived to be written down only in rural Onega, hundreds of miles distant from central Russia. There were also famous story-tellers in Onega, including the Ryabinin family, Vasily Shchegolyonok and later Irina Fedosova (1831–99) whom Gorky described in *The Mourner*.

XVI Many of the finest examples of wooden architecture are now displayed at Kizhi Open-Air Museum. The original site of the museum was the practically treeless, deserted island of Kizhi on Lake Onega. In more prosperous days Kizhi had been a busy *pogost* for the whole Spaski–Kizhi area (Spaski meaning 'The Church of our Saviour'). Representatives of both the secular and clerical authorities had their seats on the island, and indeed the two main churches and many smaller chapels and so on have survived, and a regiment of *streltsi* (a privileged military corps, developed from the infantry, founded by Ivan the Terrible in the sixteenth century) was garrisoned there. Assemblies, trade fairs and religious and other festivals were held in the town. Hundreds of peasants would arrive from neighbouring areas, filling the churches, inns and taverns, visiting government offices, law courts, schools, shops, workshops and store-houses. This *pogost*, in other words, was the political, economic and cultural hub of the whole area.

XVI, 23, 26, 27 The first of the transplanted exhibits arrived at Kizhi in 1951, an *izba* from the village of Oshevnevo, a large two-storey log house with an attic and a covered yard. A gallery surrounds the domestic quarters; beautifully decorated balconies and window-frames give the house a festive and friendly look. A single oblong framework unites the domestic and farm buildings. The living quarters, porch and entrance hall give onto the lake in the traditional way, allowing light and fresh air to flood into the house. The covered yard faces the vegetable garden. The whole ensemble is covered with a pitched roof, whose central ridge forms the dividing line between the living and farm quarters, an example of the *koshel* type of *izba*. The central point of the domestic section of the house is a spacious two-storey entrance hall with the principal (usually known as the white) staircase. The doors to the various *izbi* (here meaning living-rooms) are to the left and right of the stairs; and straight ahead a passage leads to the working part of the homestead, also on two storeys.

25 The ground floor consists of a cattle-yard with two gates, cattle-sheds, stables, store-rooms for feed and a back (or black) staircase leading up to another store-room, for hay, agricultural and hunting equipment. Here the peasants would work in bad weather, grinding corn, building boats, making fishing nets and so on. This large store-house (*povet* in north Russian dialect) is a very common feature of northern log houses. A sloping log ramp (*vsvos*), strong enough to take a horse and cart, leads outside. The upper part of the whole timber structure, above the cattle-yard, is supported by massive pillars, with their bases dug into the ground.

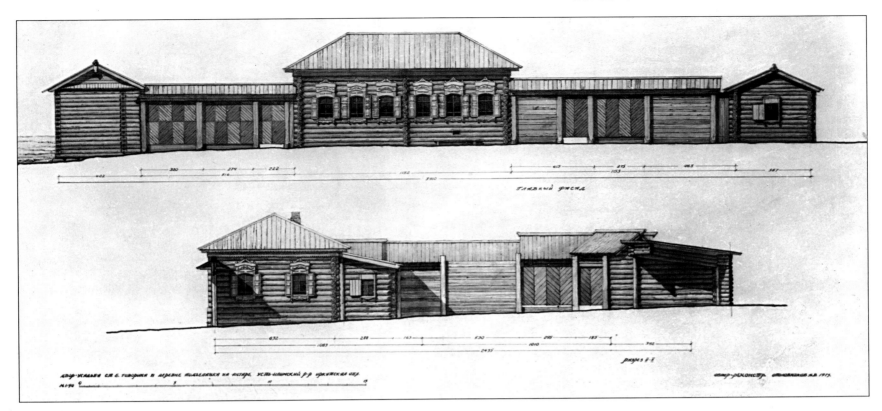

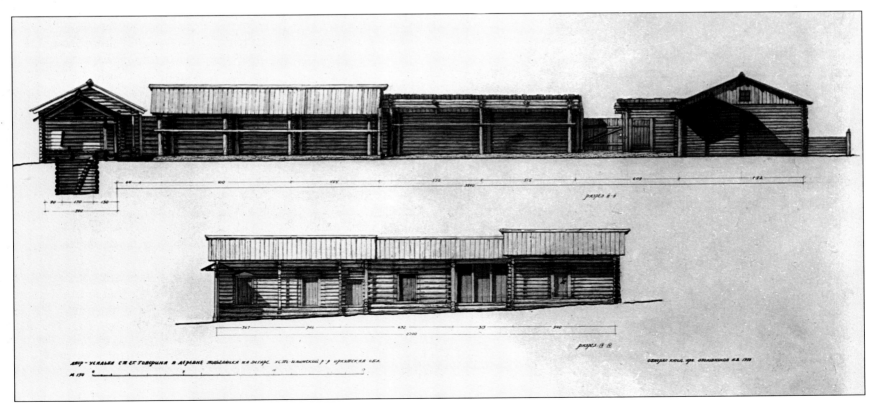

23 The house from the village of Oshevnevo (named after the Oshevnev family) restored and rebuilt at Kizhi. It is a very large peasant house of *koshel* type with asymmetrical facade, incorporating quarters for the farm animals

24 Twin windows and *nalichniki* of a house at Sheltozero, Lake Onega

25 Attic room of the Oshevnevo house, Kizhi

26 Window of the Oshevnevo house with carved *nalichnik* incorporating shutters

27 Corner of the Oshevnevo house featuring a balcony (*gulbishche*), decorative window-surrounds (*nalichniki*), a projecting console for supporting the eaves (*vypusk*) and an elaborately carved *prichelina*

28 The hook (*kokora*) of a *kuritsa* from a chapel at Korba south of Kizhi. These hooks support the grooved *potok* into which the roofing boards are slotted

This method of construction allowed the peasants to substitute new logs for any lower timbers that had become rotten without dismantling the whole house.

The Oshevnevo house contains many other interesting details typical of northern architecture and displays the marriage of beauty and function. Let us take a closer look, for example, at the roof. Strongly and safely built, without the use of a single nail, its gables are log-built right up to the top. Running horizontally from gable to gable are rough, untrimmed timbers (*slegi*) which form the main roof-supports. Athwart these, stout fir-logs (*kuritsi*) are laid. They are felled in such a way as to retain the strongest root, which then serves as a hook at the lower end of the *kuritsa*. These hooks support the grooved, gutter-like beams (*potoki*) which run along the eaves and whose grooves, in turn, receive the lower ends of the boards that make the underdecking of the roof. The upper ends of these boards are covered by the heavy, hollowed out ridge-timber called *shelom* (literally, a helmet). The *shelom* is fixed to the topmost *slega* by means of stout wooden dowels or pegs with carved tops called *soroki* (literally, magpies). Seen from a distance they really do look like magpies sitting on a roof. Though relatively small, they are very visible against the horizon and break the monotonous line of the roof.

A traceried balcony (*gulbishche*) surrounds the living quarters of the house. The original purpose of such a balcony was to gain access to the window-shutters, which afforded protection against the ice-cold winter winds and the intrusive I, II light of the 'white nights'. The shutters later lost this function and retained only their ornamental character: instead of hanging on hinges they were affixed to the window frames, becoming just a part of the elaborately carved window-frames (*nalichniki*). Their curved volutes, or scrolls, a favourite motif of the 'Russian 24, 29, 30 Baroque', were very popular in the Onega district. As time went by, the gallery also lost its functional character and became simply ornamental.

The Oshevnevo house at Kizhi is grand and beautiful, more like a fairy-tale mansion than the home of an 'unfree' peasant (though not, it should be remembered, a serf). The clear-cut forms of the powerful frame and the rhythm of the mighty interlocking logs are majestic in their simplicity. Who erected such houses? Their names are unknown but they must have been experienced builders and great artists who had a perfect mastery of their craft and a deep understanding of the beauty of simple things. The master-craftsman has always been highly prized in Russia and his fame spread far beyond his native village. (These northern craftsmen were by no means illiterate, either, as has sometimes been supposed. Indeed, in the eighteenth century, according to P. A. Kolesnikov, literacy among the males of villages in the north was much higher than in the rural areas of central Russia and some other European countries.)

The Yelizarov house is more modest than the house from Oshevnevo. The VI owner, Yelizarov, was obviously a less prosperous peasant than the master of the Oshevnevo house. The living quarters take up only one storey; indeed, they consist of just one large room for the whole family. The working section of the 31 house is smaller too. This house was brought to the Kizhi Open-Air Museum from Seredka, on the Bolshoi Klimenetsky island. It was in this village in the nineteenth century that the Russian folklorist Gilferding first wrote down the ancient legends of the Kiev *Rus*. The Yelizarov house is the oldest peasant dwelling still in

29 Part of a fanciful *nalichnik* from Velsk, Archangel Province

30 A comparatively simple type of widow and *nalichnik* on a house at Podvorya, Ivanovo Province

34

32, 33
XI

existence from Karelia. We do not know its exact date but it was certainly built in the first half of the nineteenth century. It is designed on the *glagol* plan and is possibly the last surviving *kurnaya izba* from Karelia. Smoke from the stove went directly into the living room, rose to the ceiling and escaped through a special ventilation outlet and thence through a wooden chimney-pot (*dymnik*) on the roof. The interior of the *kurnaya izba* contradicts preconceived ideas of the dark, messy, dirty interiors associated with such houses. The floor planks, timber walls, wide benches and the stove are all shining clean. The table is covered with a white cloth; the walls are decorated with embroidered cloths and articles of clothing. In the *krasny ugol* we see some traditional shiny, brass icons. Just above our heads, near the ceiling, the timbers are covered with layers of soot, but the border between the clean and the sooty parts of the walls of the *izba* is marked by long wooden shelves (*vorontsi*).

The living-room, entrance hall and covered yard of the house were built at different times. The living-room, in its present form, was built last. The entrance hall, with its own store-rooms and workshops on the ground floor, is the earliest and most interesting part of the house and preserves some rare features of the classical period of wooden architecture: small, irregular windows with inner shutters, benches with carved legs, a built-in bed for newly married couples, carved shelves for icons, massive doors and perfectly worked interior walls.

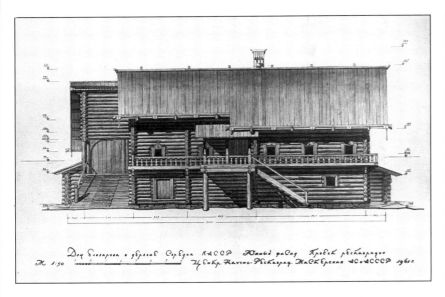

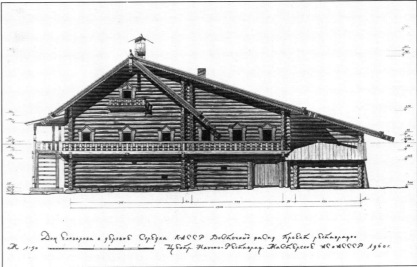

31 (*left*) The Yelizarov house from Seredka (Karelia) in a state of dilapidation before removal to Kizhi

32 Yelizarov house. Elevation of south facade with ramp (*vsvos*) for haycarts etc. on left

33 Elevation of the principal (eastern) facade of the same house. A semblance of symmetry is achieved by the false inner eave on the right. Access to the main floor to the left; entry to covered yard on right

34 Ground-floor plan of the Yelizarov house, eastern frontage below (scale for 32–4 1:50)

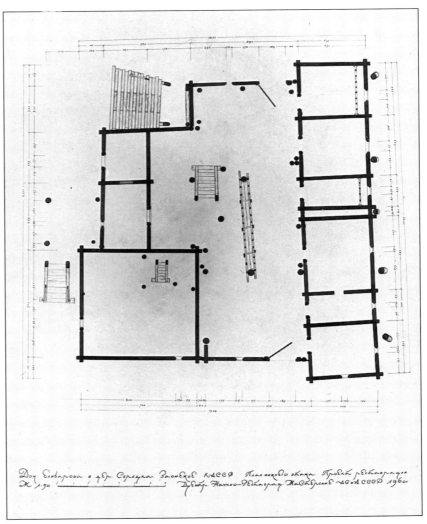

v, 35, 36

In former days there were many hamlets and small villages scattered on the shores of Lake Onega: Kuznetsy, Korba, Patanevshchina, Seredka and so on. Most of them have disappeared and only a few isolated dwellings survive. From those villages that have vanished are many masterpieces of northern Russian wooden architecture, such as the Klokov house from Patanevshchina, the Terentiev house from Petry and the Yelizarov house, preserved and displayed in Kizhi.

37, 40, 41

One of the most remarkable constructions was the Lepsin house from the village of Kuznetsy. Unfortunately it has not survived but it was studied and measured before its disappearance and we do therefore have some idea of its design and interior. This huge house occupied a dominant position on the ridge of a low hill, somewhat apart from the rest of the settlement. It was even bigger, in terms of space and of the number of separate living units, than the Oshevnevo house. Oshevnevo had four separate *izbi*, whereas the Lepsin house had five. Otherwise, the two houses were almost identical. Both were *koshel* houses built for wealthy peasant families; but the exterior of the Lepsin house was modified after it had been built and this gave it a quite different appearance from that of its neighbours. The exterior walls were faced with flat timbers and painted yellow, thus completely falsifying the original architectural design of a log building. Furthermore, the house lost its decorated gallery between the ground and first floors, its 'baroque' window frames and other characteristic features. As a result, it was so fundamentally transformed that it might have been mistaken for a stone building. Its owner was evidently trying to make it look like one of the houses of the capital St Petersburg.

Such 'modernization', whose aim was the obliteration of the ancient building traditions, became quite widespread in the nineteenth century. We might consider this process a sign of the times or a mere fashion, but this would be to mistake the effect for the cause – the drastic changes which took place in all aspects of Russian life in that epoch.

39

The Melnik house, from the village of Sheltozero, gives an impression of indestructible solidity and stability. This *brus* building differs slightly from similar constructions in having its living quarters on two storeys. Like most of the other houses in the Onega district with *nalichniki*, the domestic part of the house was built in the latter part of the nineteenth century, later than the covered yard, stables and other farm buildings. These are considerably older, being the remains of an earlier house. The window-frames (single and double) display exceptionally fine work. They recall designs in stone to be found on city buildings, and are distinguished by a specially profound sense of the balance between the parts and the whole: another two or three lines in the carved pattern and the result would be too fussy. All honour to the craftsman-architect for resisting the temptation to follow many talented local builders into the cul-de-sac of eclecticism.

The interior decoration of the Melnik house creates the atmosphere of earlier times. It is a marvellous example of loving devotion to ancient traditions. On entering the house the first thing we notice are the amber-coloured log walls with wooden shelves running along them and, in the middle of the room, a table and wide benches, also of wood. The rough walls of the oven, typical of the area, have not been spoilt by being painted in some arbitrary colour. Similarly, the floor timbers have been left in their raw state. The washstand is of copper and hangs on a copper, not an aluminium, chain.

35 Krasnaya Selga, Karelia. Traditional *izba* with 'nail-less roof', the hooks of the *kuritsi* being spaced out along the eave (compare 28)

36 Tipinitsy. An ambitious three-storeyed *izba* from this village on the main peninsula which projects southwards into Lake Onega

37   The large house at Kuznetsy (Karelia), well documented but subsequently lost. Here there was little difference between the angle of the roofs and no attempt was made to achieve symmetry by duplicating the steeper eave (compare 23 and 33)

38   Typical stair and porch (*kryltso*) of a peasant's *izba* at Bolshoi Khalui, Archangel Province

39   *Izba* at Sheltozero on Lake Onega. A more modest *kryltso* is just visible behind the fence

40   (*right, above*) Kuznetsy. Elevation of west facade. Best room with elaborate balcony on second floor. Farm animals' entry at ground level, centre

41   (*right, below*) South front of the same building. Well shown are the *gulbishche*, ornamental *nalichniki* and *vsvos*

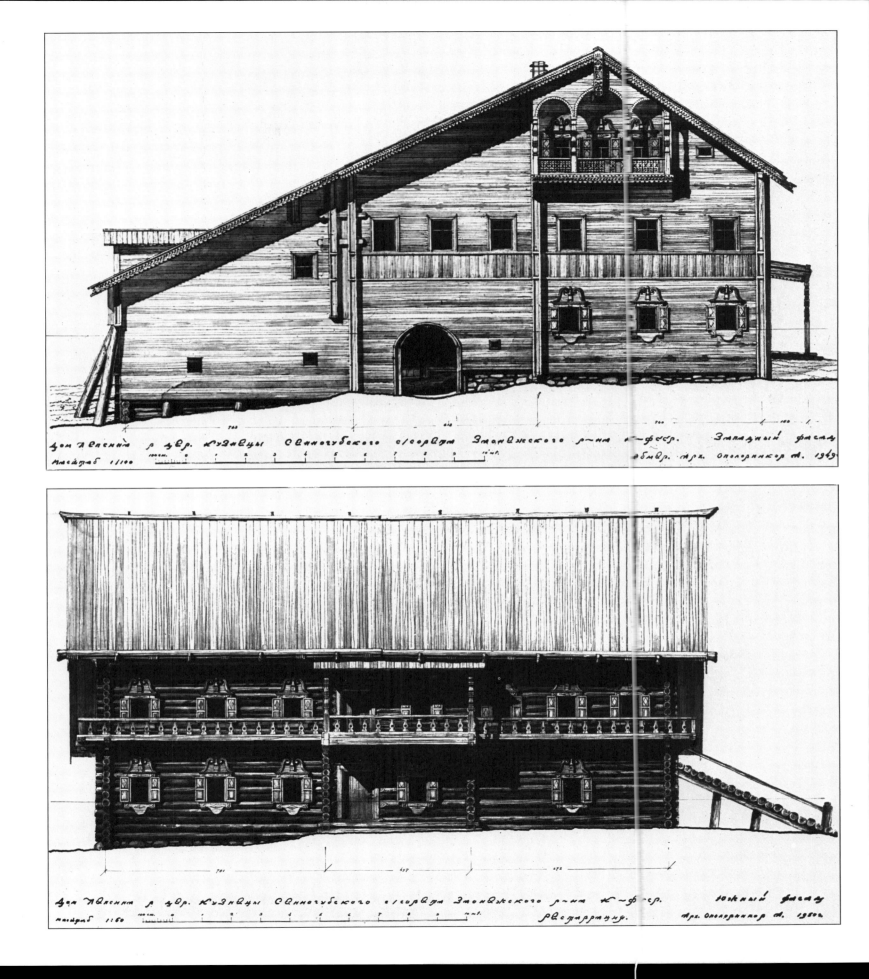

Дом Абесина р. дер. Кузнецы Сенногубского с/совета Заонежского р-на К-ф.с.с.р.   Западный фасад
Масштаб 1/100   Обмер. арх. Ополовников А. 1949

Дом Абесина р. дер. Кузнецы Сенногубского с/совета Заонежского р-на К-ф.с.с.р.   Южный фасад
Масштаб 1:50   Реставрация.   Арх. Ополовников А. 1950

Such loyalty to architectural traditions is characteristic of feudal, pre-industrial Russia. However, a considerable number of traditional peasant dwellings, especially later examples, show the strong influence of urban architecture. This tendency was particularly marked in the Onega district because hundreds of its inhabitants migrated to St Petersburg and its surroundings in search of seasonal work. Perhaps the richly adorned 'baroque' designs helped to assuage the downtrodden peasant's longing for material wealth and social independence.

MILLS

Windmills were visible from afar, erected in an exposed position not far from the main village settlement. Small villages might have one, or rarely two windmills, while larger villages, such as Azapolye, on the Mezen river, might account for up to thirty. They look like a regiment of legendary warriors, ready to defend the peasants and their worldly goods. The windmills have disappeared from Azapolye; just one survives – in the open-air museum of Maliye Korely, near Archangel.

There were basically two major types of windmill in Russia: *stolbovki* (from *stolb*, column); and *shatrovki* (from *shater*, tent). These two names illustrate two different principles of construction. In the case of *shatrovki*, only the top of the mill, with its shaft and wings, is mobile; whereas the whole body of the *stolbovki* can rotate on its axis.

Shatrovki have a massive base and are wider and higher than *stolbovki*. The latter, on the other hand, have a single-axle column supporting the main body, like a heavy head resting on a slim neck. The design gives this workaday building an unusual air. *Stolbovki* themselves are not all of a kind. Two main groups may be distinguished. The first consists of windmills built on tall supporting posts, which vary in their manner of construction and decoration. One visually impressive method of support features a high pyramid of logs (*koster*, as locals call it), laid either directly on the ground or on bearing piers. Another type of support is a simple, massive log frame built directly on the ground. Though not very elegant, mills built according to this principle are very practical. The actual working space is much larger, allowing more room for all sorts of additional equipment, such as an extra pair of millstones and a peeling or hulling mill with pestles. Such mills are usually best preserved, and certainly more common, in northern and central Russia. They display some of the original mill machinery of old Russia, made entirely of wood except for one component, a metal king-pin in the wooden millstone. A huge log serves as axle both for the wings and the transmission shaft; its bearings are the log walls themselves. Massive teeth, or cogs, are distributed along the transmission shaft. They raise and drop the heavy pestles for the hulling mill. The main (driving), toothed cog-wheel, nearly as big as the wheel of an old-fashioned locomotive, is attached to the same shaft. The cog-wheel transmits the rotation of the shaft onto a toothed drum and a vertical king-pin, and from the king-pin to the upper millstone. One such mill, from the village of Volkostrov, is on display at Kizhi. Another is to be seen at the open-air museum near Yamka.

42, 43

42–3 Post mill from Volkostrov, a small Lake Onega island, now set up at Kizhi. These vertical sections reveal its internal mechanism (compare plate XII)

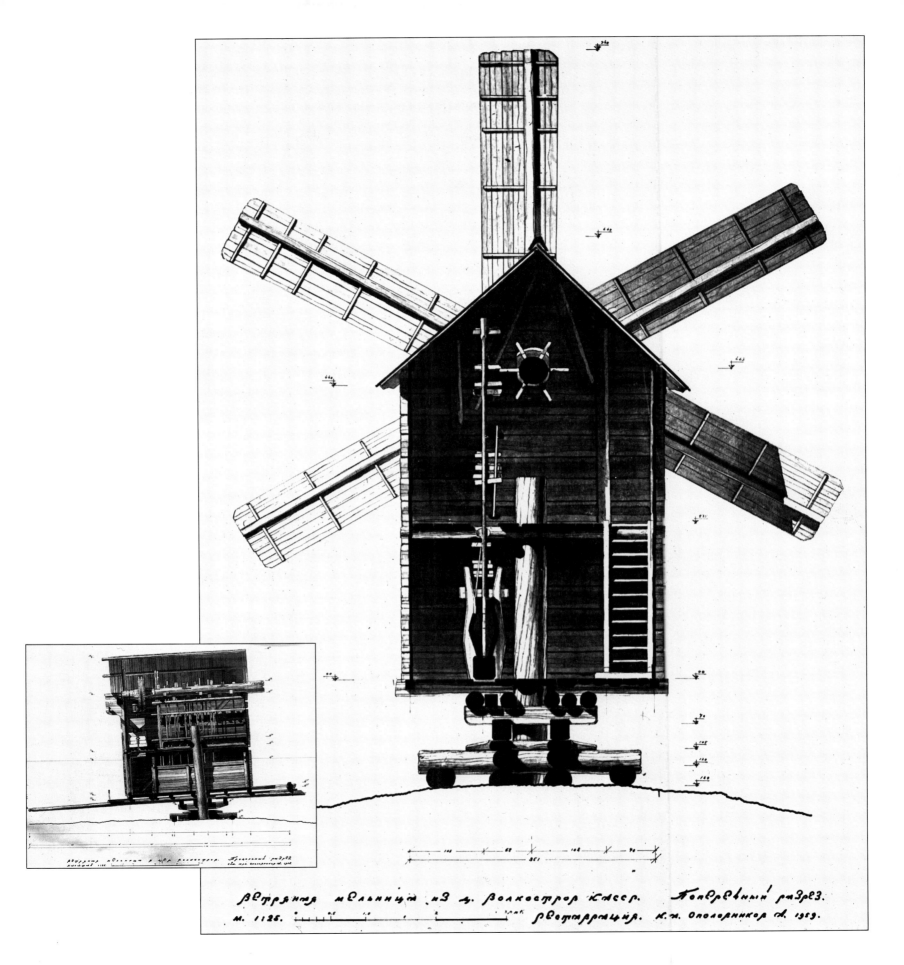

ветряная мельница из д. волкостров КАССР.   Поперечный разрез.
м. 1:25.   реставрация. к.и. ополовников А. 1959.

44 Horse-operated mill in Yakutia,
north-eastern Siberia

45 Typical log-fence in Siberia (Irkutsk
Province)

The tent-roofed *shatrovki*, also known as Dutch windmills, are not very common in northern Russia. Brought here from a totally different world, these enormous constructions symbolize new tendencies in the development of building techniques and also certain changes in the social structure of the Russian village in the nineteenth century, which was slowly adopting the capitalist forms of economic organization. The small *stolbovki*, with their restricted output, which had been a common feature of nearly every individual homestead, began to be replaced by new, huge, factory-type Dutch windmills. One or two sufficed to serve the whole village.

Horse-powered mills were also quite common in Russia in the past, though mainly in the south and in the Ukraine. They were still in use as late as the end of the last century. Some of these relics of the past can still be seen in rural parts of Yakutia, in the far north-east of Siberia. Such horse-powered mills consist of two adjoining sections: a round overhang, or roof, above the driving mechanism; and an oblong log compartment with a pair of millstones. The main component of the drive is a large, sloping, wooden gear-wheel with a shaft. The horse treads the wheel, as if continually walking uphill; the wheel rotates in the opposite direction, and the whole archaic mechanism begins to move. A large, driving gear-wheel transmits the rotation through its cogs to the smaller wheel-pulley and thence to the millstone.

In Yakutia such horse-powered mills are called 'Russian' because the tradition of grinding flour in mills, indeed the very idea of arable farming, was introduced into the area from Russia. Grain cultivation, of course, was possible only in southern parts of Yakutia, where the summers were warm and long. This is one of those rare instances when an archaic peasant building tradition, having disappeared from its area of origin, begins a new life in a similarly backward region, preserving its original form in spite of all the technical and social changes in the rest of the world.

So it was that the horse-powered mill became a monument to the craft of building and to a way of life in the history of two peoples, Russian and Yakut.

Many inhabitants of northern Russia journeyed to Siberia via the Arctic Ocean, then known as the Sacred Sea, and it frequently happened that they settled in Yakutia permanently. These people, no longer really Russian but still remaining aloof from the tribal Yakuts, spoke archaic Russian; their culture and standard of living, however, hardly differed from that of the aboriginal people around them. Explorers and researchers in Yakutia testified that many local people, even at the end of the nineteenth century, did not even know where metals and cloth came from, where flour 'grew', or how the Christian Orthodox God could rule the whole world without the aid of many spirits.

AGRICULTURAL BUILDINGS

Farm buildings, even those dating from the early twentieth century, are considered to be monuments of wooden architecture because their builders kept strictly to the ancient traditions of their craft. Though new fashions coming from the towns eventually transformed the exteriors of churches, chapels and village houses, most of the agricultural buildings were left untouched until the changes effected by the 1917 Revolution. Until that time, barns and store-houses, pole-fences, ancient mills, bridges, shooting-huts, wells and so on were being built, especially in the north of Russia, as they had been for many centuries. Everything – the plan of the building, its proportions, construction techniques and decorative detail – remained the same as before.

Store-houses in particular show many variations of shape, location and usage of space. They served many purposes: crops were stored there of course, but they also held household goods and chattels, hunting and fishing equipment and even smoked and cured fish; and were used for sleeping in the summer months. They were located according to use: fishing huts near water, those for hunting near forests. Grain store-houses, which contained the peasant's supply for the whole year, were especially carefully placed. They were always conspicuous in the landscape of the village, positioned so that the owner could keep a continuous eye on his property. They might be built next to the vegetable garden, for example, or opposite the entrance door. If homes were ranged on one side of the road, these barns were quite often placed directly opposite. Sometimes, too, barns were built on the outskirts of the village, thus creating picturesque groupings or even little alley-ways.

The exteriors, too, show the importance attached to these barns by the peasants. Carefully tailored logs; a massive door in a sturdy jamb; a heavy iron lock with a decorated keyplate; and modest ornamentation on the *prichelini* and pillars, all create an impression of strength, durability and aesthetic unity.

The interior of the barn was no less carefully and lovingly done. The main elements of the granary are long, tall container-bins (*suseki*). These are built into the log frame itself. They are solidly made of broad, thick timbers, tightly joined to avoid any waste of grain. Cleverly designed compartments separate flour, groats and grain and regulate their constant flow from the bins into vessels for

46–7 Counterpoised wells, as seen universally in eastern Europe and other parts of the world. Both are at Verkhnyaya Uftyuga on the River Uftyuga, a tributary of the Northern Dvina

48   Hinge from a barn door at
Rudakovo, Archangel Province

49   Barn door-grille, Irkutsk Province,
Siberia

50–51   Consoles or brackets for eave
support (*vypuski*) from Siberia (dated
1844) and Archangel Province

52   Field barn at Purnozero, Karelia,
with ends of *slegi* jutting out
conspicuously under the eaves. A
characteristic of older barns is that the
walls curve outwards, as here, so
increasing the protection afforded by the
eaves

immediate use. These *suseki* are usually only on the ground floor of the granary, along its right and left walls, with a gangway in between them. There are no windows on this level and light only penetrates when the door is open.

The upper floor was normally used for storing leather and pelts, yarn, clothing and all sorts of small articles. A tiny window, a mere slit in the wall with a thick iron grill, hardly dispels the darkness of the room.

Another special feature of such store-houses is a very strong, reinforced double ceiling: beams under the roof are placed close together and also interlock with the log walls. This construction protects the contents from intruders as well as from rain and snow.

The huge locks on the barn doors are worthy of attention, in particular the sophisticated mechanisms with their unique 'secrets' and individually decorated key-plates. The keys for such locks are massive and can weigh up to four pounds. The handles are finely wrought with ornamentation round the shafts.

To ascertain the age of a barn we need only examine the log-ends where they interlock at the corners. If they have been cut with an axe, rather than sawn, the barn is old, built in the ages before the eighteenth century when cross-cut saws were rarely to be found in villages. Sawn logs rot much more quickly than those cut with an axe because sawing produces an even cut, thus increasing the permeability of the wood, leading to earlier rotting. In addition to their practical advantage, axe-cut logs are more attractive: their contours are varied and look more natural than monotonous, cross-sawn log-ends.

Another indication that a barn is of venerable age is the presence of a *poval*: this is a widening or overhang of the upper part of the log rectangle outside, under the roof, into a cantilevered bracket or console. Its purpose is to enable the roof to be spread wider, the better to protect the walls from snow and rain. The aesthetic qualities of the *poval* are evident: it lends a flowing air and an elegant flourish to the facade of the barn. There are barns whose artistic qualities put them among the finest examples of wooden architecture, though they cannot, by their nature, rival the elegant homes and elaborate churches which dominate them.

It is rare to find two identical store-houses in one village. Even if they are of the same type, they are sure to have some individual features. They may be of one or two storeys, with an internal or external staircase, with or without a *poval* which may or may not be supported on pillars. The entrance may be at the front or at the side, and the roof and ceiling may have one or two sloping surfaces and be single or double. They may be detached or semi-detached, raised above the ground on

53   Field barn with nesting box at Ustya, Kalinin Province (formerly Tver). As in 52, the *slegi* show up clearly

54   Double barn with correctly constructed nail-less roof at Turya, Komi Autonomous Republic. Two hooked ends of *kuritsi* support the grooved horizontal *potok* which in turn supports the lower ends of the roofing boards

55   Thatched barn at Myt, Ivanovo Province

supporting columns, or else built directly on the ground. The grain containers may be on one or both sides.

The hunting and fishing store-houses, as well as the community barns (forerunners of shops), all had their peculiarities. Take, for example the little barn from the village of Pelduzhi, now on display at Kizhi. One detail of its construction changes the whole appearance of the building – the special method of attaching *potoki* without the use of *kuritsi*. There are many more such examples: all of them show great variety of silhouette, proportion and ornamentation. Their external appearance is always determined by the character of the local settlement and its architecture.

KARGOPOL HOUSES

As well as Lake Onega there is also a river Onega. It rises in Kargopolye, near Lake Lach, and flows from south to north, embracing within its two tributaries, the Karelski and the Dvinski, its native earth, Onega itself, before flowing into the White Sea. The town of Kargopol is situated at the source of the river, and it was from here that Russian influence began to spread into the north of the country. Records of the town go back to the fourteenth century, and in the *Kniga Bolshomu Chertezhu* (The Great Book of Designs) of 1627, the classic work on Russian fortifications, it is designated the 'glorious city of Kargopol'. In 1380, Prince Gleb of Kargopol, with other princes of the area, responded to the appeal of Dimitry Donskoy to defend the Russian homeland against the Tatars. Gleb died a hero's death on the ensuing battlefield at Kulikovo. By the seventeenth century the whole Onega area was under the control of the military governor of Kargopol, but within a hundred years its importance as a regional centre had declined.

56   Wooden smoke-stack of a
kurnaya izba or 'black house' at
Gar, Kargopol District, with
A. V. Opolovnikov

57   A *kurnaya izba* from Gar rebuilt
in the Maliye Korely open-air
museum near Archangel. It is an
obsolete type of peasant's house with
no internal chimney

58   (*far right*) A more modest
example of the same type of dwelling
at Gar

59   Stove and kitchen equipment of a
kurnaya izba

This happened to all the other northern cities. The city lost its independent status and came under the successive authority of the provinces of the once Swedish Ingermanland (including St Petersburg), Novgorod and, after 1801, Olonets. Nevertheless, the traditional ways of life and building were respected and preserved by local people.

56, 57   The Tretyakov *kurnaya izba* in the village of Gar (Kargopol district) was visible from afar. The outline of its massive wooden *dymnik* stood out clearly against the bright background, towering above the other houses. Its unique, exotic shape fascinated and excited the enthusiastic researchers who rediscovered it in the 1960s and had it transferred to the Maliye Korely Open-Air Museum. It had remained in its original state for hundreds of years. Inside, the smooth logs making up the walls were of a golden-amber tint. Wide, clean benches ran along the walls whose upper, smoke-blackened parts were separated from the cleaner timbers below by *vorontsi* shelves. A traditional Russian stove without a chimney stood under the soot-laden ceiling, which was reinforced by massive tie-beams. The original system of protecting the inhabitants from the effects of smoke was still in place: the high, trapezoid ceiling collected all the smoke without troubling those below. The soot would be regularly and carefully cleaned off, especially before religious festivals. The original smoke-flue survived intact in its position above the entrance door. It consisted of a long, narrow opening which could slide open and shut. A wooden channel drew the smoke to the *dymnik* on the roof which, as explained above, protected the whole system from rain, snow and wind.

59   The Russian stove stands, huge and unpainted, displaying all the natural beauty of its wooden housing and the confident draughtsmanship of a true folk artist. Such stoves are nowadays as rare as *dymniki* and are mostly to be found in the Kargopol area.

This system of 'chimney-less' heating determined, to some extent, the design of the whole building. To begin with, the height of the *kurnaya izba* must be such that the smoke would always remain far above the head of the people below, that is, at roughly the same level as the ceiling of a house with a conventional method of smoke extraction. Accordingly, the ceiling and the upper parts of the walls of the *kurnaya izba* must be high enough to increase the volume under the roof. As a result, the *kurnaya izba* is usually three or four log-widths higher than a conventional *izba*. The high facade, together with the *dymnik*, is a tell-tale sign of an old *kurnaya izba*, even if the original, chimney-less stove has been transformed into a conventional one. The other typical feature of the *kurnaya izba* is its trapezoid ceiling, also for smoke extraction.

58   There were many such houses in the Kargopol area, either identical to the Tretyakov house or slightly different, but all exemplifying the *brus* type of construction favoured by the Onega region builders.

The earliest known survivor of this type of construction may well be a house in the village of Gorka on the River Onega. The date of its completion, in 1811, is carved on the lintel of the entrance door. The individual character of its architecture and its present pathetic condition confirm the age of the building. True, in the course of its long life this homestead has lost half its covered yard. Its

60
61   living quarters have deteriorated and some parts have completely disappeared. But enough remains for us to appreciate its interesting design and to allow us plausibly to reconstruct the missing elements.

In its original state this was a typical *brus* building: a massive, oblong log framework under a wide, overhanging gabled roof with carved *prichelini* and a heavy *shelom* ending in the shape of a horse's head. A large wooden *dymnik*, the inevitable accompaniment to every *kurnaya izba*, completed the picture.

As usual, only the living-room with its stove faced the river and the street. The house was entered at the side, through a raised porch resting on two carved pillars. A large room gave access to the living-room through a door on the right; another door, on the left, led to store-rooms and small, heated winter quarters, and thence to a two-storey covered yard with stables and animal-pens. The ramp for the horses led upstairs, where there were haylofts and more store-rooms.

Some unusual features of the house are characteristic of the Onega region. A partition, into which the stove is set, divides the living-room. The stove opens into

60   Stove in an *izba* at Gorka, Archangel Province

61   Window-grille, Gorka

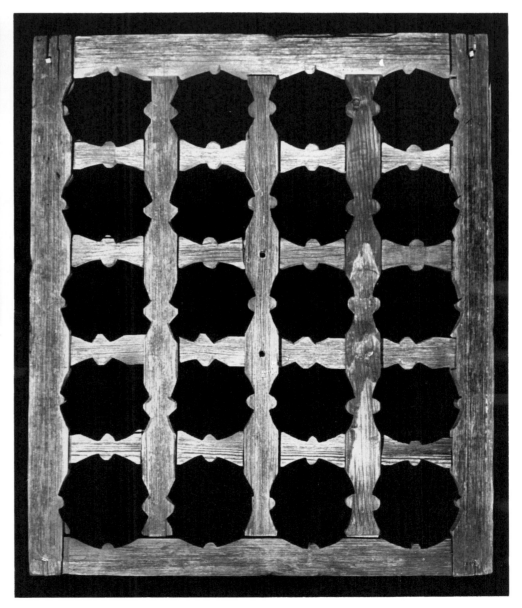

the larger section, the *izba*, which has three windows facing the road. The smaller section (*prirub*) has only one window and a double ceiling, and is warmed by the heat from the back of the stove. So the *prirub* was the warmest and cleanest room in the house, isolated from all the smoke and soot. It is often described as the white *prirub*, a later development of which was the *gornitsa*. The latter, a large, airy, light and spotless reception room decorated with icons, was separated from the rest of the house by a solid log wall. This, the 'fifth' wall, gave its name to a particular type of house, the *pyatistenok*.

Another feature of this house is an extra, smallish living-room with a stove – a miniature *izba* – used as additional winter quarters. This room, known as the *zimovye* (from *zima*, winter), was either located separately, next to the yard and animal-pens, or else, as in this case, was integrated into the main building on the southerly side of the working quarters. The northern side was taken up by store-rooms; a corridor in between ended in a staircase which led up to the haylofts.

The builder obviously attached no small importance to the entrance hall. An ornate shelf in the corner bore the icons. The edging and legs of the benches were finely carved, the banister supports carefully turned. The ceiling was constructed in two layers, the lower layer consisting of timbers laid with a small gap between them. The logs making up the wall were as smooth as the massive door-jambs. An internal shutter was attached to the sturdy window-frame. A bed for a young couple was ingeniously built into the wall. This entrance hall is a now rare example of the sort of work which was once commonplace all over the country. Northern Russia is the last refuge of the old traditions of wooden building, which arose in the princedoms of Novgorod, Tver and Vladimir–Suzdal and were brought thence to the virgin lands by the early pioneers.

62 Village of Kalgachikha, Archangel Province, with two bath-houses down by the water

63   Zharky, Kostroma Province. Bath-houses raised on stilts in a floodable area

PINEGA VILLAGES

In the countryside round the River Pinega, the eastern and largest tributary of the Northern Dvina River, villages, surrounded by thick forest, are scattered along the river banks. Fyodor Abramov, born in the Onega region, wrote in 1977: 'In winter, the Pinega villages, veiled in snow, deep in the forest, look all alike. In spring, as the snows melt into the roaring streams, each begins to show its face. One, like a bird's nest, clings to a steep hillside. Another perches so near the edge of the high river-bank you could fish from the window. A third, immersed in grassy waves, hearkens all summer long to the grasshoppers' free concert in the meadow.'

Larger villages were usually situated like little islands in the driest and most convenient spots, connected by waterways or simple tracks, cut through the vast, uninhabited forest. They spawned daughter villages, consisting of a few summer cottages and tiny sheds for storing food and personal belongings; they were without the big farm buildings such as mills, threshing barns or granaries to be found elsewhere. The peasants would stay there all through the summer and autumn, until the first falls of snow. They were always busy, grazing their animals, cutting and storing hay; and there were mushrooms, berries and herbs of every sort to be prepared for the winter.

The summer cottages of the village of Ust–Ulesha on the Pinega can be counted among the simplest and earliest examples of the *brus* type of log building.

73

64   Interior of a bath-house at Khornima, Archangel Province

They were quite primitive and very cramped. The log ceilings were low and soot-blackened. The tiny shuttered windows had no glass, and a very modest door, with a twisted bough for a handle, swung on crude wooden hinges. Wide benches along the interior walls were used as seats during the day and as beds at night. The chimney-less stoves were made of a mixture of clay, straw and gravel. The outsides of the huts were devoid of all decoration and gave the same rough-and-ready impression as the interior, hardly different from a hunter's hide. The walls were bare, with the ends of the logs left irregular and untrimmed at the corners. The roofs were almost flat and the roof timbers were kept in place without the aid of *kuritsi* or *potoki*. Smoke-pipes made from hollowed-out logs were sometimes present. A few simple outhouses were scattered about.

Such a village might be thirty kilometres or more from the main settlement in an area, with virtually no roads suitable for wheeled traffic. If it could not be reached by boat the only method for transporting heavy loads was a primitive horse-drawn contrivance consisting of two strong poles, joined at one end, on which hay and so on was laid; in the winter sledges were used.

By the middle of the nineteenth century chimney-less stoves were obsolete, but bath-houses continued to be heated by the same principle for another hundred years. If the village was far from water, the bath-house was put in the back yard. If at all possible it was built by the side of the river or lake.

The bath-house was an oblong log cabin under a single or double sloping roof. Inside, just to the right of the threshold, was the primitive stove, just a pile of burnt and soot-covered stones on a low base, arranged in a sort of crude arch, under which the logs were placed. As the stones heated, smoke rose to the ceiling and went out through the door, which was left slightly ajar.

64   Nowadays, large coppers are fitted between the stones to obtain hot water, but the traditional (and very effective) method was simply to toss the hot stones into tubs of water. There were two wide benches along the left and far walls and a 'sweating-bunk' above, for those who enjoyed their bath very hot. Bundles of birch twigs were used for massage. Large water tubs, a basin, a bucket, a ladle and a pair of iron tongs made up the contents of the bath-house. There was a small, unheated extension for dressing and undressing. The traditional bath-house kept its original character and appearance long after other village buildings had lost theirs and even now you will find steam baths being built in the old way in rural areas in the north of the country.

HUNTING CABINS

Hunting was an essential part of the peasant economy. It provided food, clothing and a cash return. The hunter's primitive cabin seems to be an organic outgrowth of the invincible forest in which it is set. From outside it looks like a simple, casually built log hut under a single or double sloped roof, with a small door and a tiny window. It contains only a chimney-less stove, broad benches or bunks and, instead of a table, a wide board fitted to the wall near the entrance. A few shelves provide storage for crockery and provisions; a pole, high up under the ceiling itself, is used to spread out wet clothing and skins and, when the hunter is away from the cabin, anything which may be damaged by rodents or other animals.

IX

65, 66

65   Hunter's hut (*izbushka*) on the River
Ileksa, Archangel Province

66   Hunter's hut on the River Kata,
Irkutsk Province, Siberia

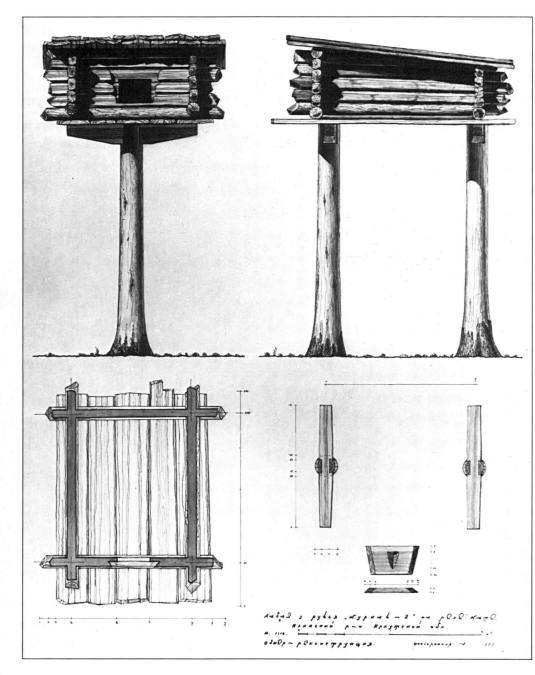

67   Restoration of the hunter's store (*labaz*) near his hut on the Kata. It is raised on legs as a protection against marauding wild animals. Front and side views and structural details

68   Hunter's log table by his hut on the River Voloshka, Archangel Province

69   A hunter's store-box for food and skins in Karelia

70   Hunter's store raised on very tall posts, by a stream joining the River Kata, Irkutsk Province

Custom dictates that any passer-by in need of sustenance or shelter may use any provisions, such as salt and tea, as well as wood for the stove, which he finds there. He, in his turn, is expected to leave the cabin clean, tidy, stocked and ready for the next occupant.

68   A few yards in front of the cabin is the picnic table, a simple board on a structure of interlocking logs, the two lower rows of which serve as benches. The local name for this is *lava*. (The same sort of table, up to five metres long, can be found outside summer cottages, where a whole village might sit down to eat 67, 69, 70   together.) A previously common feature, now more rarely seen, is a diminutive store-house perched on one or more poles, up to three metres high, to protect food, game, furs and skins from foraging animals and rodents, in the absence of the hunter.

Although the huge forests might seem an undivided vastness to the outsider, there was in fact a strong and enduring sense of territory and even ownership between and within villages. To guard against the occasional theft, hunting cabins were discreetly situated or even concealed; only a few initiates might be familiar with the secret paths leading to them. The hunter would place traps along the paths connecting his cabins, which were usually a day's march from one another. They would be stocked with victuals and equipment in the summer, brought there by horse or boat. People consciously sought attractive spots for their cabins: the local soubriquet for them was 'the jolly places'. Nowadays, the old conventions are in decay. The animals which used to be hunted are now being bred. Hunting has ceased to be a livelihood and has become a sport; and modern cabins are being built which owe nothing to the past. It is rare indeed to come across a set of original hunting structures cut with the axe. Unfortunately, there are no pictorial records of these humble objects and it is difficult for us in the twentieth century to imagine their original appearance.

BRIDGES

Techniques of bridge construction remained unchanged in northern villages for centuries; indeed, specialized carpenters were building them at the time of the Kiev *Rus*. Until quite recently these bridges, large and small, could be seen over many northern rivers and streams, some of the longest extending for more than a hundred metres. The most remarkable were built on cribs, or rectangular, log 73   piles filled with stones. This was the only possible method of spanning the hard, stony river-beds with their fast-flowing currents. Rows of baulks, or bearers, consisting of three or more sturdy logs laid on top of each other, were placed lengthwise above the piles. An unbroken, crosswise layer of shorter logs formed 72   the actual thoroughfare of the bridge. It is amazing now to see heavy lorries, powerful tractors and trailers trundling across these rather dilapidated bridges, which have withstood the tremendous spring currents for centuries.

In the village of Ovchinkonets (Archangel Province) the bridge over the River 71   Kena rests on five log piles. Its age is uncertain but we do know that the route to Novgorod has passed through here for hundreds of years. More recently, in the

71 Fedorovskaya on the Kena (a tributary of the River Onega) and its remarkable log-built bridge

72 Bridge near Pochozero south of Onega, western Archangel Province. One of hundreds of small log bridges in the north

seventeenth and eighteenth centuries, the riverine settlements belonged to the large local monastery, which enjoyed widespread economic relations with many parts of Russia. The bridge, therefore, was an important link in the network of roads. No doubt it has been renovated regularly and new logs have been substituted for rotten. Old people in the village claim that it has been completely rebuilt in a slightly different position every fifty years or so.

This type of bridge, which has survived only in Onega, has a very ancient ancestry. The 'Great Bridge' over the River Volkhov in the city of Novgorod itself was mentioned regularly in contemporary chronicles, at least from 1133, recording damage caused by flooding, storms and especially floating ice during the spring thaw. The Great Bridge must have been continually improved and strengthened.

Such bridges also play their part in the aesthetic and architectural unity of the landscape. They represent the horizontal plane, while the churches rise in perpendicular splendour; with ancient dwellings and chapels, mills and barns, all clustered round the lofty banks of the stony Kena, they create a unique spatial harmony and constitute the essence of the medieval Russian wooden village.

SIBERIAN HOMESTEADS

The borders of the Moscow *Rus* began to expand rapidly in the second half of the sixteenth century. It took less than fifty years for Russians to cross the Urals, conquer Siberia and reach the shores of the Pacific. The fortified settlements they built all over the vast new territories are constantly mentioned in seventeenth-century official documents. Nikolai Spafariy, the first Russian ambassador to China, is particularly prolific on the subject. In those days the settlements, *zimovye*, were used mainly in the winter, because it was only possible to travel for long distances then, using the frozen rivers rather than the thick, virgin forests which were virtually impassable.

Domestic buildings still to be found in Siberia fully preserve the best traditions of European Russian wooden architecture, which is not surprising since they were built by Russian colonists. Local traditions, however, also left their mark. The peasant homesteads of western and eastern Siberia have one thing in common: they are completely enclosed, little fortresses on permanent alert, very different from the open-plan, fenceless, hospitable groups of houses, with domestic and agricultural buildings gathered under one roof, to be found, for example, in the Onega region. Life in Siberia was quite different from the easy-going existence in Mother Russia. Settlers had to be on their guard against bands of exiled and escaped criminals and rebels. The indigenous population was also frequently hostile. To protect themselves against sudden attack the pioneers constructed strong, high fences, heavy gates and houses with shutters which could be made fast with iron bars. A row of closely built store-houses and other farm buildings, without a single window facing the street, rendered the inner courtyard impregnable.

A quite different type of homestead is to be found in eastern Siberia, by the River Angara. A splendid example is the Govorin house in the village of

73 Log bridge over the River Churega, Archangel Province

74 Verkhnyaya Uftyuga on a tributary of the Northern Dvina. Its footbridge across the river and, in the distance, the 'tent' of its wooden church

75–7

75 Village of Aksinino on the River Angara, Irkutsk Province, Siberia

76 Eave support (*vypusk*) from an *izba* in the same region

Podyelanka. The domestic *izba* is joined to two distinct courtyards: the first, 'clean' yard contains granaries, barns for keeping clothes and equipment, ice-houses for storing food, even rooms for summer sleeping. The second, working enclosure has stables and animal-houses, haylofts and hen-coops. The facade of the whole homestead, fifty metres long, runs beside the river.

'An Englishman's home is his castle' is the saying that comes to mind as we gaze on the buildings by the Angara. The difficult and dangerous life of the settlers forced them to take every possible precautionary measure. Now the necessity has vanished but the tradition, exemplified in these fortified buildings, lives on.

Siberian forests were almost limitless and produced many different types of wood. Builders were adept at suiting a particular wood to the function required. The lower three log-courses of a basic rectangular structure, for example, were usually of larch, which is relatively impervious to wet ground and melting snow. In Yakutia, ancient churches on the rivers Indigirka and Alazeya, built entirely of larch, have survived to this day, their log frames quite untouched by wet rot. This wood was also used for any parts of the building vulnerable to rain water, condensation and damp, particularly ceiling joists, gutters, *shelomi*, high roof-beams and gate-posts. Inside, larch was also used for bathrooms and cellars.

The logs above the layers of larch were usually of pine, which was 'warmer' and easier to use. Pine was preferred for the central section of the framework, as

77 Aksinino on the Angara. These comparatively modest single-storeyed *izbi* could be almost anywhere in northern Russia or Siberia

well as for floor and ceiling planks. *Kuritsi* were made from fir and roof tiles were of silver fir. Siberian pine, clean and smooth, was used for gates, window- and door-frames and the interior of the *izba*. Five different woods in one *izba*! Today such fastidiousness might seem a luxury but in those days it was everyday practice. In the north of European Russia, similarly, the basic rectangles were of pine, fir was used for the structural details of the roof and aspen for the silvery domes of churches. Nature's abundance and occasional scarcity dictated the rules; the result has been centuries of survival against the elements.

It seems there are only two forces that can destroy these buildings: fire from lightning and man. Today we can install lightning conductors and as for man, we can well understand the tragic consequences of losing our inheritance. The traditions of our forebears offer us stability and the enlightenment which flows from understanding the past.

3 · Fortresses and Fortified Towns

Tell the world:
Russia lives! We welcome you all!
But remember!
He who comes with his sword unsheathed shall die by the sword!
This is the eternal principle of our great Russia.

THESE are the legendary words of the defender of the Russian homeland, Prince Alexander Nevsky (1220–63), who succeeded in pacifying Russia's troublesome neighbours by a combination of military might and peaceful deeds. As the nineteenth-century historian S. M. Solovyev wrote in his *History of Russia*: 'Alexander's lasting glory lives on in his defence of Russia against the Eastern threat and in his heroic feats in the West in the service of faith and country.' The Orthodox church reveres Alexander Nevsky as a saint. His life epitomizes the struggle to establish a centralized Russian state, a process in which the longing for independence went hand in hand with the search for peaceful co-existence with the rest of the world.

The history of Russia is a painful one but even during periods of the greatest hardship its people have preserved its freedom and independence. Legends, poems and songs glorify their patriotism, bravery and heroism in war. This strain of heroism also runs through medieval Russian folk architecture.

'We may be sure that it was a feeling for beauty which dictated the construction of the earliest and humblest log buildings, let alone the city walls and towers which mark the beginning of our architecture', wrote I. Zabelin in 1900. The analysis of wooden fortifications is difficult for the simple reason that hardly any such structures have survived to our day. They began long ago to fall into decay as the need for them disappeared. In central Russia they vanished far earlier than in the north – in Siberia especially they were still being built at least until the middle of the eighteenth century.

Of the numerous mighty, wooden fortified structures spread around this vast country only a few wooden towers and other buildings have survived into the twentieth century. These, with ancient drawings, prints and written records, allow us to recreate the appearance of a medieval Russian wooden town. A

80

78   Reconstruction of a 'powerful wooden fortress on a high river-bank' of the 16th century. Based on Totma on the River Sukhona, a main tributary of the Northern Dvina

powerful wooden fortress rises on a high river-bank. Its massive walls, grim and impregnable, warn off the most confident enemy. Pointed towers stand, eternally vigilant, at every corner. Elaborate church domes and large houses complete the unmistakable picture. At the fortress's foot a river flows or a lake spreads out and all around, as far as the eye can see, fields, meadows, forests . . . Mother Russia.

In medieval days any fortified position was a *gorod* (from the verb *ogorodit*, to surround with a fence or wall). As time went by, however, the concept of a fortress merged with that of a settlement and *gorod* took on its modern meaning of a town or city. Contemporary chronicles tell us that wooden fortified towns, such as Novgorod, Polotsk, Belozero and Rostov the Great, were being built in the ninth century, at the very dawn of the Russian state. Stockaded settlements were sometimes built at strategic border-points, but they were manned and occupied by military detachments only in time of war.

The many monasteries which sprang up as Christianity spread through Russia in the tenth century were also built with an eye to defence. For many centuries the land knew no peace. Aggressive neighbours, warring princes and invasions from east and west all meant danger to villages, towns and even remote monasteries. Abbot Daniil, describing wooden monasteries at the beginning of the twelfth century, informs us that they were built as fortresses, and many chronicles bear witness to their impregnability.

79

84

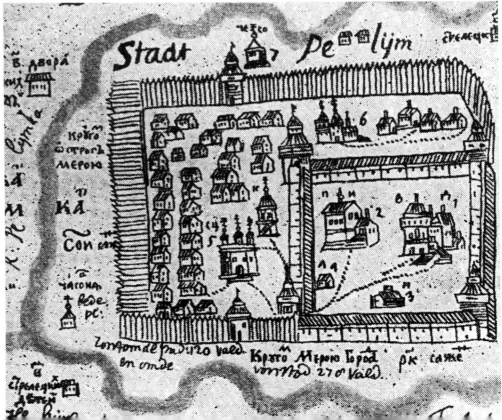

79 The ancient city of Novgorod 'the
Great' on the Volkhov, drawn about
1635 by Adam Olearius (from
*Beschreibung der Muscovitischen und
Persianischen Reise* 1656). Near right:
the stone-built kremlin and Cathedral of
St Sophia. Beyond the river: the 'market
side' with its wooden walls and houses

80 A 17th-century sketch of a fortified
settlement, Pelym, where the River
Pelym joins the River Tavda, east of the
Urals, Siberia

The high standard of fortified wooden building later manifested itself in stone. (A perfect example of this is the Solovetsky Islands monastery in the White Sea, whose gigantic walls and towers are built of huge stones weighing up to eight tons each. Three centuries after its construction in the 1580s it was able to withstand the siege of an English fleet.) Wooden fortifications could not possess such strength and naturally decreased in number as military technology, and especially artillery, continued to develop. The hundred years from the 1350s to the 1450s were critical for all Russian military science, including the art of fortification. Firearms began to replace bows and arrows, spears and javelins, but wooden fortresses continued to be built for many years and their towers and strong log walls went on stubbornly withstanding enemy attack. The roar of the first cannon sounded the death knell of wooden fortification which in the seventeenth and especially the eighteenth century could no longer resist the new military techniques. Its place was taken by complex stone structures built according to the latest discoveries in engineering. Fortification became a specialized subject engaging the attention of highly skilled technicians very different from the old-fashioned carpenters of the past, who could turn their hand to any task.

LOCATION AND HISTORY

In Siberia it was different. Wooden fortifications continued to be built until the middle of the eighteenth century and in arctic Siberia a hundred years after that: a wooden fortress was built on the River Maly Anyui, a tributary of the Kolyma, as late as the end of the 1840s. Siberian tribes, unfamiliar with firearms at the time of the Russian colonization of their land, found such wooden fortresses so unassailable that many were never used for the purpose for which they were built. Even the fortress of Yakutsk, with its sixteen towers and double walls, was in practice unsuitable for significant military actions, but it presented a formidable appearance and testified to the might of the Russian State.

The construction of the Siberian fortresses was the last chapter in the history of wooden defences. Subsequent changes in the Russian economic system, as well as the growth of trade and cultural contacts with other countries, prepared the ground for the great reforms instituted at the end of the seventeenth and the beginning of the eighteenth centuries. These reforms, identified with Peter the Great, stabilized the nation and strengthened the international position of the Russian state. They mark the demise of the medieval *Rus* and the birth of the new Russia.

In spite of the vast distances which separated these wooden fortresses, they show few differences in their basic design. The reasons for this are not hard to fathom. Firstly, they were all built of a common material, wood; secondly, they used traditional but highly functional and practical methods of construction that had been preserved for many generations. Finally, and most significantly, they were all constructed to house similar military equipment.

The fortresses and monasteries, placed like sentries among the disparate Russian princedoms, played a very important part in uniting them into a single, multi-national political entity centred on Moscow. They were built where trade

129

routes met, on important waterways, at the mouths of rivers and at other strategic points; but always with good views of the surrounding countryside, to avoid the danger of being caught unawares by an enemy approaching the walls. They were generally built in elevated positions or else in low marshy areas where no forests or ravines afforded natural protection to the enemy.

Geographical location, as well as differing levels of economic development, determined the number and position of fortresses in the various princedoms of Russia. In the years between 1200 and 1450 Russia fought no less than 160 major battles: 45 were against the Tatars, 41 against Balts, 30 against Germans and the rest against Swedes, Poles, Hungarians and Bulgarians. Two areas in particular developed strong defensive systems early on: one in the north-eastern, the other in the north-western part of the country.

By the 1360s the rulers in Moscow had intensified their efforts to unify the Russian princedoms. This policy brought to an end the lack of co-ordination in fortress building. Indeed, the strategy and planning of new, fortified towns became an important element in the history of Russian unification.

The city of Moscow was the first to modernize its defences. By the end of the fourteenth century a solid ring of monastery–fortresses surrounded the 'mother of Russian towns': Andronnikov, Simonov, Zachatyevsky (the Immaculate Conception), Rozhdestvensky (the Nativity), Petrovsky and Sretensky (Feast of the Purification).

Vasily the First, Grand Duke of Moscow (1384–1425), ordered the defences of the town of Pereslavl to be rebuilt in 1403, and followed this with the building of several new fortified towns: Rzhev (1408), Pless (1410), and Kostroma (1416). The other princedoms also increased their military defences and the ending of the feudal wars (1425–53) led to the establishment of centralized power in Moscow.

The process of unifying the Russian state only came to an end at the close of the sixteenth century, when the Boyar Republics of Pskov and Novgorod, as well as the Grand Duchies of Tver and Ryazan became subordinated to the rule of Ivan III, the first 'Tsar of all the Russias'.

The conquest and retention of new territories required the creation of more and more fortified towns. As frontiers changed, so some of the old towns lost their strategic and military importance and developed into centres where trade and crafts could flourish. Those fortresses in the northern and western marches of the country, however, increased in importance.

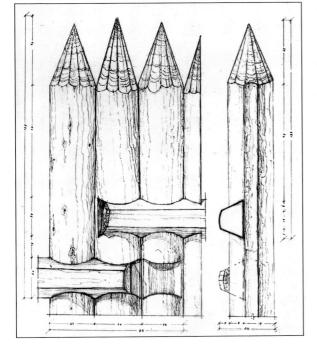

81   Reconstructed detail of an early stockade, as used for fortified positions in the 15th and early 16th centuries

CONSTRUCTION

Even in pre-Christian times, up to the tenth century, the Slavs had surrounded their settlements with stockades made of vertical, pointed, solid logs. Such a stockaded village was called an *ostrog*, from the word *ostriy*, sharp. Contemporary chronicles relate that the height of the fence depended on the presence and size of any other defences such as ramparts, moats or fosses. If the ramparts were high and the ditches deep, the stockade would be built only to the height of a man's chest and the fight would be conducted over the stockade or through the narrow gaps in it. The stockade itself acted as a sort of parapet, protecting the warriors rather than the fortress. If there were no earthworks it might be five to seven metres high, either dug into a low mound, or else directly into the flat earth.

Sometimes the stockade was set at an angle. These slanting stockades were most common in Russian settlements in Siberia, especially in the north-west, probably because the permafrost there made digging particularly difficult. Seventeenth-century examples are to be found on the Indigirka, Alazeya and Ochota rivers.

As firearms became more widespread these simple methods of fortification became ever more complex. The first improvement was the introduction of embrasures at chest level. Later a second row of embrasures was added at ground level; and a log platform was fixed to the inside of the wall so that the defenders could fire over the top as well. The platform, supported by diagonal or lateral struts, was reached either by a ladder or by a single log with steps carved into it. One such stockaded settlement was built as late as 1704 in the northern Kamchatka peninsula.

Packing the space under the platform with earth was an extremely efficient method of strengthening the stockade. This may be considered an early stage in the development of a more advanced method of fortification, that based on a log shell or *srub*.

Fortress walls constructed of a series of such rectangular divisions, all filled with earth or stones, were known as *gorodnya*. They are recorded as early as the eleventh century. The chronicles also describe the continual repair and rebuilding of these fortifications, as rain-water and melted snow collected between adjacent frameworks, rotting and destroying them. This was work of the utmost importance because, before the widespread use of firearms, the high, solid walls provided a thoroughly effective means of defence and usually obviated the need to fight.

The length of any one log rectangle in the *gorodnya* depended on the size of the available logs, and its thickness varied according to whether the enemy were using spears, arrows and battering rams or whether it was cannon and firearms that had to be blocked. Walls facing open land without any natural or man-made obstacles had to be even more powerfully reinforced.

An improved method of construction, known as *tarassa*, did away with separate log compartments. Two solid log walls were built, with cross-walls at regular intervals, about every six to eight metres. The first recorded example dates from 1553; they were probably in existence a good deal earlier, though perhaps not under the specific name *tarassa*.

Generally, each section of the *tarassa* was packed with earth or stones. If, however, there were embrasures at ground and chest level, extra 'floors' would be built and only the space between was filled in. Some sections, with a door let into the inner wall, and embrasures in the outer wall, were left hollow. A variation of the *tarassa* was to build alternate sections as triangles filled with earth and stones; the others were left hollow to allow defenders to shoot at the enemy from the shortest possible distance. The walls of the fortress of Krasnoyarsk, built in 1628, are among the rare surviving examples of this method.

The thickness of the *tarassa* varied from 1½ to 4 metres. Usually, its height was augmented by a sloping roof, which created a kind of attic, or gallery, with rows of embrasures set into its double walls. This extra space was called *oblam*. Benches were installed in it so that the upper row of embrasures could be reached by the defenders, who could fire from a reclining, kneeling or standing position. Holes were let into the overhanging part of the roof, for pouring boiling water or tar (and anything else to hand) over attackers who had managed to reach the walls of the fortress. (Another stratagem was to fix huge logs at the top of the roof and release them at a critical moment in the battle, thus crushing the enemy to death.) A defensive gallery of this type was built onto the fortress of Korotoyak in 1648. This particular fortress is distinguished by its use of vertical and horizontal rows of pointed stakes to dissuade the enemy from using ladders to overwhelm the settlement.

97 Watch-towers were built on high, open locations inside and outside the fortified town. They were called *vezhi* (from *vedat*, to know). They were square, hexagonal or octagonal, the latter being the most effective from the watchers' point of view. They were topped by a pyramidal roof. These *vezhi* are recorded as early as 1159: 'The *vezha* towers high above the town and all four corners of the earth are plain to see . . .' The tall, gaunt towers became a symbol of independence and patriotism for the Russian people and their characteristic silhouette is a recurring motif in other wooden as well as stone architecture.

Although the earliest watch-towers might be placed either inside or outside the walls, later towers were built into the walls themselves. They are referred to as *bashnya*, the modern term for towers, in sixteenth-century records. The basic
93, 94 principles of their construction hardly differed from that of the walls. They were generally on two floors with a row of embrasures on each level. Like the walls, they possessed an overhanging roof and an *oblam*, usually somewhat higher than the walls. Access was gained by an internal staircase or, if the tower were small, by a ladder or external staircase. Most fortresses also had a higher, multi-storey tower with a turret.

Fourteenth- and fifteenth-century towers were concentrated on the forward walls where most military activity might be expected. These walls were longer
104 and more massive than those to the rear and sides. In time this differentiation disappeared and by the seventeenth century walls on all sides were built equally
82 strong, with equidistant towers placed all round the perimeter, irrespective of any river, lake or forest which might offer natural protection to attackers or defenders. With an astute use of firearms defenders could create a field of fire round the whole fortress and a 'dead' zone which an attacking force would find almost impossible to penetrate. Sometimes an additional obstacle to the enemy's
97 progress was placed round the citadel: a deep, wide ditch, filled with water or bristling with pointed stakes.

The earlier fortresses, with their concentration of towers on the forward wall, give out a sense of dynamism and tension, of alert watchfulness, while the later rhythmical alternation of vertical towers and horizontal walls, combined with large homogeneous surfaces and a mass of detail, created a pleasing, flowing, sculptural, even monumental effect, which is a striking feature of all the wooden architecture of the time.

These Russian fortresses were imbued with a sense of dignity and strength which symbolized the age which gave them birth – the heyday of the Muscovite state, which was confidently stepping onto the world stage. The creation of a stable independent state, able to cast off the chains of Tatar servitude and then to

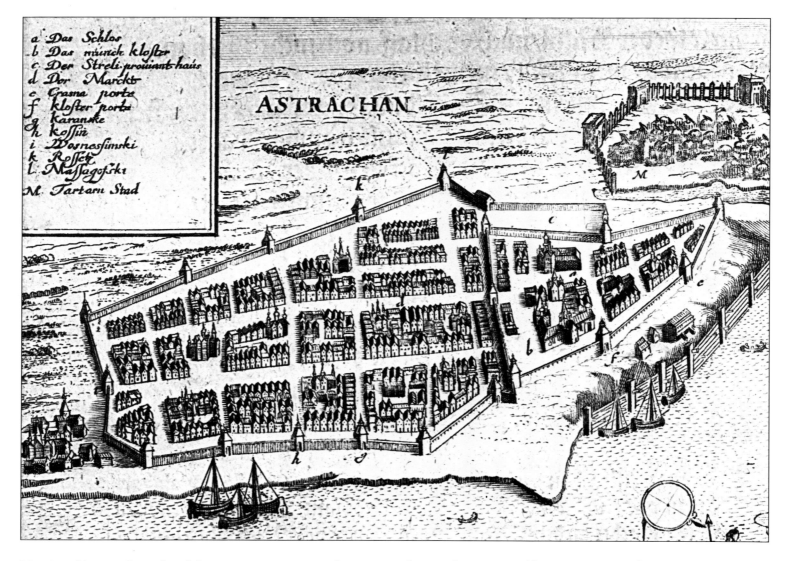

a Das Schlos
b Das münich kloster
c Der Streli:proviant:haus
d Der Marckt
e Crasna porte
f kloster porte
g karanske
h kossin
i Wosnessimski
k Rossch
l Massagofski
M Tartarn Stad

ASTRACHAN

82 Astrakhan in the Volga delta near the Caspian Sea. Upper right: the Tatar settlement with its own defences. Most of the timber needed for the town's construction would have been floated down the Volga from more northerly regions (from a German engraving)

conquer the previously terrifying Tatar khanate, imparted to its people a new enthusiasm and energy, a renaissance in all areas of life.

PLANS AND MODELS

As the power of the Russian state grew, its towns also increased in strength. Many had two or three rows of walls, with some sections of stone and others of wood. The wooden *Bolshoi gorod* of Novgorod the Great had two named stone towers: the Alexeyevskaya and the Pernovskaya. The stone fortresses of Vologda, Tula, Serpukhov, Novgorod, Kazan and Astrakhan were surrounded by wooden walls. The *kremlin* or citadel of Tula, for example, had an additional wooden stockade

82

built around it in 1673. This was a double wall with a roof of sawn timbers. There was a gate-tower at each corner and fourteen defensive towers were dotted round the walls. A secret passage led from one of them, the so-called water-tower, to the citadel itself, enabling drinking-water to be brought in during a siege.

A fortress had to be built within a limited period of time and in accordance with architectural drawings sent from Moscow. It had to conform to a budget and quantity survey laid down by order of the Defence Inspectorate. The drawings were rather schematic and thus the more important document was the survey, which gave a detailed description of the dimensions, any special features required, the materials to be used and the workforce to be employed. Interestingly enough, the architectural plan issued from Moscow never took topographical factors into account and had, therefore, to be considerably adapted in each individual case.

Occasionally a maquette or model of the proposed fortress was issued along with the plan. For example, in October 1649 the Governors of the Olonets fortress, F. Volkonski and S. Yelagin, sent the Tsar, Alexey Mikhailovich, a report on the renovation of the fortifications 'enclosing the survey, architectural plan and model of the fortress'. Even earlier, in 1623, a carpenter by the name of Savka Morozov was awarded a grant of a bolt of cloth 'for his fine work in making a model of the Kaluga fortress'. The tradition of model-making continued for centuries. A model of the Church of the Evangelist at Ishna is done to a scale of 1:16 and in nearly every big Siberian town you will come across models of the original, local fortified settlements. These models were based on the definitive study of the subject published between 1699 and 1701 by S. Remezov, *Chertezhnaya Kniga Sibiri* (Siberian Architectural Drawings and Plans). Plans and drawings of all the major fortified towns erected by the Russians in the vast Siberian territories by the end of seventeenth century are included in Remezov's book. Remezov evokes the grandiose and ambitious sweep of the architects of earlier times and their achievements in the face of the harsh Siberian conditions.

SIBERIAN FORTRESSES

The surviving fortresses of Siberia are our best clues to Russian fortifications as a whole. In central areas of Yakutia, for example, we find some of the smallest:
83–6 fortified store-house towers, originally built by Russian colonists in the seventeenth century to protect their winter settlements, and later copied by natives of the region during their own tribal wars. When the Yakuts began to build fortresses for themselves they did the job so well that even Russian artillery could not overpower them. A good example is the little fortified store-house by the mouth of the River Aldan, belonging to one Nikolai Sleptsov. It had triple walls, with the half-metre gap between each wall packed with earth; the outer wall had two rows of embrasures. The ceiling was also triple; it lay on huge beams
87–9 reinforced with iron. The double doors of the fortress were similarly reinforced.

83–4 'Barn fortresses' at Kyolba, Amginsky District, Yakutia. The flush corner-jointing in 84 indicates a comparatively late (18th century?) date

85 Kyolba, Yakutia. Upper chamber of the same or a similar barn fortress

86 A fortified store-house or tower-barn now at Cherkekh, Yakutia, north-eastern Siberia. Similar buildings were ancestral to the more sophisticated defensive towers adopted later.

87   Barn fortress at Biekino, Megino-
Kangalasky District, Yakutia. The upper storey
is the look-out post from which shots could be
fired

88   Double-shuttered door of the Biekino
barn fortress

89 Biekino. Detail of timbering of the same building

In peace-time such a fortress would have been used for storage or as summer quarters. If an enemy threatened, the occupants simply barricaded themselves and their belongings inside the massive perimeter.

As in Russia, so too in Siberia fortifications were built on high, open locations so that a watchful eye could be kept on the surrounding countryside. One of the oldest surviving examples is the tower built by one Ponomarev. It consists of a rather low, rectangular base surmounted by an attic under a pyramidal roof, a rarity in Yakutia where most fortified towers have flat roofs, often made of turf. The Ponomarev tower, a six-metre cube, with sixty-eight embrasures in its four walls, never grew into a large stockaded town. Its roof calls to mind some of the most ancient tent-roof wooden churches in Russia, such as St Nicholas in Lyavlya, St Vladimir in Belaya Sluda and the Church of the Transfiguration from the village of Spas–Vezhi (now displayed at the Kostroma Open-Air Museum). A similar tower was built at Anyuisk, one of the most remote corners of north-eastern Siberia (*see below*, under Eastern Siberia).

Nearly every Siberian *ostrog* began life as a winter settlement to accommodate the Russian newcomers in warmth and comfort. (We must not forget that 'winter' in Siberia means the months from September until May.) From the outside, the simplest version of a winter settlement resembled a hunting lodge, being a basic

90, 91

222

129

90 Ponomarev tower, Maia, Megino-Kangalasky District, Yakutia. Fortress-tower and look-out point, 17th century (?). The restored section shows two upper rooms reached by ladders

91 Ponomarev tower. The angled pyramidal log-roof, well seen in the absence of boarding, is unusual in Siberia

kurnaya izba. Closer inspection, however, reveals double ceilings and walls, with embrasures cut into the latter. One such settlement, built at the end of the sixteenth century on the River Lyapin (a tributary of the Irtysh, itself a tributary of the Ob) was only rediscovered at the beginning of this century. It had grown into an *ostrog*, which was later destroyed, leaving only the original *izba*. Ivan Rebrov, the explorer who discovered the Rivers Yana and Alazeya, reported in a dispatch to Yakutsk, the regional administrative town, that he 'had built a fortified and turreted winter settlement on the newly discovered Yana.'

In north-eastern Siberia these turreted winter settlements were known as 'Cossack fortresses', or 'Cossack towers'. Gerasim Ankudinov, one of the most celebrated explorers of Siberia, built one of these Cossack towers, which later grew into an *ostrog* and thereafter into the large arctic settlement of Middle Kolymsk. The 'tower' survived until the end of the last century.

EUROPEAN RUSSIA

The sixteenth century in European Russia, internally divided and beset by enemies beyond its borders, was the golden age of fortress building. After the battle of Kulikovo in 1380 it seemed that the Tatars had been finally defeated but Russia was to experience only a short period of peace. Forays and incursions into Russian territory were very frequent even before the foundation of the khanate of Kazan (1438–1552). The long wars with Turkey (1677–81, 1687–1700), which continually encroached on Russian soil, were particularly burdensome. In the west the ancient foe of Russia, the German Teutonic Order of Knights, persistently attempted to weaken Muscovy by denying it access to the Baltic Sea and thus isolating it from Western Europe.

Under these circumstances the rulers of Russia were clearly obliged to pay special attention to the defence of the state. Vast sums of money and an enormous amount of labour, skill and ingenuity were devoted to the strengthening of far-flung borders. A strong line of defence was created in the south, consisting of the fortress-towns of Livni (1586), Voronezh, Kromi, Yelets (1592), Oskol (1598), Belgorod (1593), Baluiki (1600) and others. At about the same time a number of fortresses were constructed on the banks of the Volga, among them Chorniy Yar, Tsaritsyn and Samara.

At the end of the sixteenth century the majority of fortresses in the central region of the country were still of wood; the few citadels built of stone were to be found in the capital, Moscow, in the Alexandrovskaya *sloboda*, and in Tula, Kolomna, Zaraisk, Starytsa, Yaroslavl, Nizhny Novgorod (now Gorky), Belozersk, Porkhov, Novgorod and Pskov.

One of the most noteworthy features of Russian military architecture in the sixteenth and seventeenth centuries was the creation of unbroken lines of 'field fortresses' (*zaseka*). They were made up of felled trees, roughly piled to obstruct the enemy; earth ramparts surrounded by stockades of sharpened stakes; ditches and moats; trous-de-loup (camouflaged holes, with sharpened stakes at the bottom to give a most unpleasant surprise to the unsuspecting invader); and small fortresses built of oak and pine, with watch-towers, platforms for cannon, guard-rooms and barracks. As well as these man-made devices, full use was made of any natural features, such as rivers, swamps, dense forest and so on, which might deter the enemy. In the steppes, for example, ditches and ramparts were dug and fortified on high ground wherever possible, in order to slow down the legendary Tatar cavalry. These fearsome horsemen could only be resisted if they were forced to a more moderate pace. Then their attacks could be successfully repelled by firearms and cannon strategically placed on the fortress walls.

The tradition of defence lines has a long ancestry, in fact: a continuous defence system was built as early as the tenth century in order to strengthen the southern borders of the Kiev *Rus*. Bruno, a German missionary, passed through Kiev on his way to convert the Pecheneg (tribal Tatars) to Christianity in the first decade of the new millennium. He tells us that Prince Vladimir, Grand Duke of Kiev, 'defended the borders of his territory with strong stockades extending over a wide area, about two days ride from Kiev in all directions.'

One of these defence lines, built at the end of the sixteenth century, stretched along the River Oka for seven hundred kilometres, from Nizhny Novgorod via

Serpukhov to Tula and Koselsk. Between 1635 and 1653 the Belgorod defence line, one thousand kilometres long, was constructed, extending from the River Vorksla to the River Chelnovaya. A large number of towns sprang up, populated by *streltsi*, Cossacks (pressed into service from the border guards) and by men and women from every walk of life. Among these towns were Kozlov, Tambov, Korocha, Userd, Yablonov, Volny, Khotmyzhsk, Kostensk, Karpov and Nezhegolsk. A chronicle relates: 'An earth rampart, 12 versts long [1 verst = 1.06 km] begins at Kozlov . . . three fortresses, with towers, are built along it . . . in the same year, the town of Tambov was built on the River Tsna to protect us from the depredations of Crimean and Nogayan Tatars. Soldiers are quartered there. The rampart from Kozlov to Tambov is further fortified by stockades made of sharp stakes . . . another two fortresses have been built beyond the town of Shatsk, on the River Lomov: Upper and Lower Lomov by name . . . thanks to these new fortified towns and the older fortresses of Ryazh, Ryazan and Shatsk, our area is now strong enough to repel the Tatar invaders.'

In 1647 the Korsunskaya, Atemarskaya, Tetushchskaya and Zasurskaya defence lines, in the central Volga region, were begun. In 1654 the line westward from Simbirsk (now Ulyanovsk, the birthplace of Ulyanov–Lenin) was built. It connected more than ten fortresses (such as Urensk, Sursk, Atemar, Korsun) and reached the fortified line round Tula.

The war against Poland for the Ukraine (1664–66) necessitated the construction of a defence line between the fortresses of Velikie Luki, Smolensk and Opochki. The fortress and defence line of Suzran was built in 1683. The breadth of all these well-guarded defence lines was impressive. They were, on average, two to three kilometres wide; in areas of dense forest they could be up to sixty kilometres wide.

An enormous amount of effort was expended on the huge defensive ring stretching between four great Russian rivers, from the Dnieper and the Don to the Volga and the Kama. Any one building-site engaged the labour of up to ten thousand workers a year. By the end of the seventeenth century hundreds of thousands of people all round the country were working on the obligatory construction of such defence lines. It eventually became a crushing burden, not only on the civilian, tax-paying population, but also on hitherto privileged groups among the military. *Streltsi* and Cossacks, for example, now found themselves having to contribute compulsory labour to these ambitious projects.

IMPROVEMENTS

The border fortifications of Russia along the White and Barents Seas were being continually improved and increased all through the seventeenth and into the eighteenth century, and especially during the Northern War. The old fortresses of Kola, Suma and Kem were thoroughly modernized and new ones built. These too were of wood, for the building of stone fortresses, although already widespread in the western and north-western regions of Russia, was rare in the north, where wood remained the basic building material, especially in the remoter forest areas.

95–7

The years 1583 and 1584 saw the building of the town of Archangel, on the Northern Dvina near the White Sea coast, as both fortress and safe haven for shipping. The wooden walls of the town went down to the river itself, whose banks were also strengthened. The high level of construction skills and the painstaking joinery exhibited at Archangel, as well as other fortresses, aroused the admiration of all who came to visit.

These new citadels and fortified towns were erected mainly in the border regions of Russia. In central Russia it was more a matter of modernizing old fortresses whose crucial defensive significance had decreased. A list of towns drawn up in 1678 informs us: 'A new citadel is to be built at Kaluga. New citadels have already been built at Kostroma, Mtsensk, Belev, Yelets, Vyazma, Murom and Pereyaslavl–Zalesky. The old town of Stariy Oskol was burned down and was replaced with a new one in 1630 . . .'

The old Russian fortresses, whether of wood or of stone, were marvellously expressive and beautiful: foreigners admired them and Russians were filled with pride as they gazed on them. Boris Godunov, observing the erection of the kremlin at Smolensk is reported to have said: 'We will build here a work of such beauty that it will be without compare under heaven. . . . the wall of Smolensk will become a priceless jewel adorning Russia . . . the envy of our enemies and the pride of Muscovy.' When danger has threatened, the 'sober, spiritual intellect' of the Russians (A. Tolstoy) has known no limits. Witness the well-nigh incredible tale of the tower, thirteen metres high, built and fitted out with cannon and all the paraphernalia needed for a full-scale siege, all in the course of a single night. And not in some remote forest but at the very gates of the enemy fortress of Kazan.

Ivan the Terrible's campaign in Kazan in the year 1550 had ended unsuccessfully. Contemporary chronicles attribute the failure to bad weather and in particular 'the tremendous rains, which prevented the taking of the city'. But the Tsar himself, supported by his soldiers, refused to put the blame on external factors but instead on the absence of Russian fortresses round Kazan. For this reason it was decided to build a citadel fifteen *versts* away from the city 'on the Round Mountain between Shchuchye Ozero [Pike Lake] and the River Sviyaga'. In the spring of 1551, with not a moment to lose, according to the Chronicle of Nikon, 'the Tsar called his Scribe, Ivan Grigoryev, son of Vyrodkov, and dispatched him, with other Boyars' sons, to the Volga, to the Ushaty domain, in the district of Uglich, there to construct churches and fortresses, to dismantle them and ship them thence, down river [some 640 kilometres by water] under military escort to Kazan.' And so it was that, a mere four weeks later (according to the legendary tale in the chronicle), 'a brand-new wooden town, cunningly designed' arose at the mouth of the Sviyaga. The walls were of the *tarassa* type with several rows of embrasures, including one at ground level. Seven towers, each of three storeys, loomed over the seven fortress gates, which were reinforced with iron. Secret underground passages had been built into the fortress in case of siege: one led to the Sviyaga and another to Shchuchye Ozero. The citadel, 'of the utmost splendour', as Nikon says, had been worked out to the last detail.

The final, victorious Russian campaign against Kazan took place in 1552. The citadel was taken by storm. Just before the attack, Russian engineers first erected the aforesaid tower, thirteen metres high, in a spot well away from the enemy's prying eyes, then dismantled it and covertly transported it right up to the Arsky gates of Kazan itself. It was re-erected overnight. Accurate artillery bombardments opened the way for the *streltsi* regiments to advance into the city. Kazan yielded, and the whole Volga, from its source to Astrakhan, belonged to Russia thereafter.

This story highlights a unique feature of wooden architecture, namely the ability to dismantle and re-erect a structure in a short period of time. There are marvellous tales of fine churches miraculously floating to their final resting-place, but fairy-tales always contain some nuggets of truth, for churches were indeed constructed where wood was plentiful and shipped to their intended destination.

FORTRESS POPULATIONS

The population of fortresses was determined by their size and location. In central regions their make-up was overwhelmingly civilian, while soldiers were more numerous in the border areas, where there was a marked absence of the upper and lower nobility. Ordinary people, too, were unwilling to abandon their land and homes to move to the new, dangerous regions and commandants frequently complained to Moscow that they lacked civilian volunteers to live in the new settlements. Border fortresses were originally manned only intermittently but by the end of the sixteenth century they were being guarded round the clock and all year long, and the seventeenth century saw soldiers, 'together with wives, children and all their belongings' being transferred to these outlying posts permanently, if necessary by force. This marked the beginning of regular garrisons in border areas, which became firmly established in Russia by the end of the eighteenth century.

THE PLESS FORTRESS

For centuries, frequent Tatar raiding parties destroyed the peace and prosperity of the population of the Upper Volga. In 1237 Baty (1208–55), the grandson of Genghis Khan (*c.* 1155–1227), led a cavalry invasion thousands strong into Russian territory. After bloody hand-to-hand battles the cities of Ryazan, Vladimir, Moscow and Kiev fell one after the other, fatally weakened by disunity and division. A year later the Upper Volga region was ravaged and laid waste, and 'its people were taken into slavery and their goods and chattels stolen', as the chronicles put it. The Volga was a very convenient route into Russia, but its banks were stubbornly defended by the Russians, whose bravery was legendary among the Tatars: 'They are swift as eagles and fear not death. One Russian will brave a thousand invaders, two Russians will take on ten thousand.'

92–4 In 1410, according to the chronicles, 'Prince Vasily Dimitrevich, Grand Duke of Muscovy, ordered the construction of the fortress town of Pless on the upper bank of the Volga, on the eastern border of his princedom. In the same year Yedigey, the bloodthirsty prince of the Golden Horde, attacked and devastated the riverine and maritime towns' (those along the Volga and around its mouth, where it flowed into the Caspian Sea).

92 Pless, on the upper Volga, Ivanovo Province. Site of the old wooden fortification as it now looks

93 Pless. Reconstruction of one of the smaller towers of the fortress, with plan and section

94 Pless. Ground and upper-floor plans of a hexagonal tower, reconstructed. The hexagonal form was much less common than the octagonal

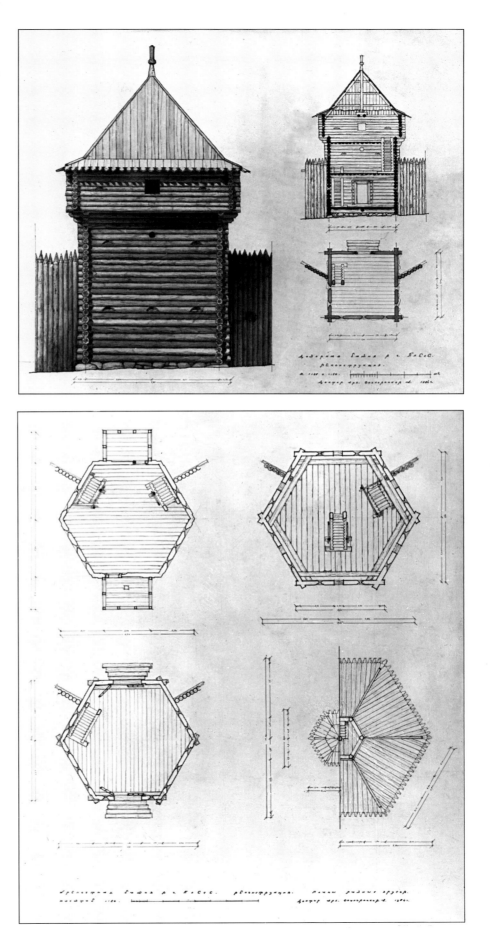

92

The Pless fortress was built on a steep slope near the mouth of a small, but in those days navigable, river called the Shokhonka. It was fortified with ditches and ramparts. From the top of the hill there was an excellent view of the surroundings and, most important, of the straight course of the Volga. In fact, Pless takes its name from the word describing a straight stretch of river.

Two guard-posts were placed at the approaches to the town to provide early warning in case of attack. One was just opposite the fortress itself, the other a few *versts* down river, half-way between Kineshma and Kostroma.

It is difficult for us to picture the appearance of these guard-posts: nothing now survives except their names. They may have been small fortresses with watch-towers, surrounded by a stockade; or they may have resembled the Siberian fortified winter settlements or the Cossack towers described earlier. The wooden fortress of Pless itself has completely disappeared; only the steep hill and its mighty ramparts remain. However, an informed picture of Pless can be

93, 94

constructed: its pointed stockades of massive oaken logs bristle like a watch-dog. They are riveted together on the inside by dove-tailed wooden beams and further reinforced by an embankment of earth and stones. The highest watch-tower, commanding a view over the Volga, stands in the south-east corner of the fortress, with smaller towers spread at intervals around the perimeter.

A wooden Church of the Assumption stands in the centre of the fortress, where nearly three centuries later, in 1699, a stone church with a tent-roofed bell-tower was erected in its place. Next to it is the military governor's house, then food and ammunition dumps and, in the north-western corner, barrack huts for housing the garrison.

There are two gates into the fortress. The northern gate leads to the Volga, the western over a bridge spanning a deep moat, and thence to a small *sloboda* named Holy Trinity after its church. The gates are guarded twenty-four hours a day and closed at night. The clang of heavy chains raising and lowering the massive bridge would have disturbed the evening hush which enveloped the valley of the Volga.

We do know that the living space of each man was strictly regulated according to rank. In the comparable town of Userd, for example, built in 1637 on the River Tikhaya Sosna (Quiet Pine), every Cossack was entitled to 5×3.5 *sazhen* (1 *sazhen* = 2.13 metres) and every *strelets* 4×3 *sazhen*. In the fortress of Pless, however, as in the rest of Russia, there were no such divisions among other ranks until the middle of the sixteenth century.

The staple firearm used in Russian fortresses was the hand-held musket (sometimes called *ruchnitsa* from *ruka*, hand). There were three variations of this weapon: one was used for defence, another for attack and the third (*sokoliki*, little falcons) was used by guards stationed outside the fortress. Bows and arrows were still very much in use in the fifteenth and into the sixteenth century. An archer who could not hit his target twelve times a minute was considered 'unworthy of his honourable calling'.

In 1429 a great Tatar army led by the Khan of Kazan, Mahmoud Khazi, plundered and razed many of the towns along the Upper Volga, among them Lug, Kineshma, Soldoma, Pless and Kostroma. The chronicles tell us that 'the Tatars of Kazan attacked the fortress of Galich, in the domain of Prince Yuri Dimitrevich, without warning. They remained there a whole month. At Christmas they came a second time and devastated Kostroma, Pless and Lug and escaped down the

Volga. . . .' After this disaster the fortress of Pless was rebuilt, but following a few years of uneasy peace Pless was involved yet again, from 1434 to 1458, in a long feudal war between the princedoms of Moscow and Galich, the latter under the rule of Dimitry Shemyaka and Vasily Kosoy. Moscow refused to pay tribute to the Tatars in 1462, and from then on Pless became an assembly point for Russian armies defending their homeland from the depredations of the Golden Horde. It was at Pless in 1540 that the Tatar army suffered its greatest defeat. This battle was one of the turning-points in the Russian struggle for independence.

Before the victorious campaign against Kazan in 1551 and 1552, Ivan the Terrible had ordered a military detachment to be formed at Pless. In 1552, joined by regiments from Kostroma under the command of the Princes Gorbaty and Serebryany, it took part in the capture of the city of Kazan. Another Tatar stronghold, Astrakhan, fell to the Russians in 1556, after which the whole of the Volga, from its source to the Caspian Sea, was liberated. This was not the end of war on Russian soil, however, and loyal Pless shared the often cruel fate of the motherland.

Pless did not lose its military importance until the first quarter of the seventeenth century. Its wooden fortifications were burnt down during the 'Time of Troubles' (1605–13) and never rebuilt. It later became a busy manufacturing and trading centre. War finally passed the city by and the mighty hill where once the fortress stood now bears the name Mount Freedom.

KEM, SUMA, KOLA

The leading fortresses in the chain of defence protecting Russia's northern borders were Kem, Suma (on the White Sea, south-east of Kem) and Kola on the Barents Sea. All were of wood. Their *tarassa* walls were the finest product of contemporary military technology and stood the test of time and many fierce battles. Even in the eighteenth century, when the use of firearms and artillery had become universal, this design, strengthened by earth ramparts, proved quite as effective as many stone fortifications. One indubitable advantage of *tarassa* walls was the relative simplicity of their construction and the speed with which they could be built.

Kem is a town on the coast of the White Sea, adorned by the splendid Cathedral of the Assumption, built in 1711. The wooden fortress, however, was built much earlier. The remains of one of its towers were noted by Suslov in 1888. The tower was leaning badly and seemed on the point of collapse, but it proved easy to find traces of fortifications dating from the sixteenth and seventeenth centuries. The history of Kem is closely bound up with the history of the Russian north. In 1450 Marfa Boretskaya, the elected governor of Novgorod, granted the town of Kem to the Solovetsky monastery. By the end of the sixteenth century the monastery was in possession of the entire district round the town, 'together with the Muzer monastery, salt-works and mines, the local peasantry and exclusive rights to game and fish'. In 1657 a wooden, stockaded town was built on a nearby promontory, the isle of Lep, to protect the area against Swedish and Norwegian invaders. This citadel, equipped with cannon and arquebuses, was the mighty fortress of Kem.

95, 96

The one tower that survives is impressively large. We may assume that the whole building was on a grand scale, only comparable with the fortress of Yakutsk. The tower, as usual for the time, was a double-walled structure, with the space between the walls filled with earth and stones: a forerunner, in fact, of the *tarassa*. Suslov wrote in his study of the area: 'The huge octagonal leaning wooden tower of the old citadel leans over the end of the promontory, its ancient fortifications long since washed away by the currents of two lusty rivers. The daughter church of the old Solovetsky monastery can be glimpsed behind this mute witness to battles of bygone days. The hillside is dotted with a few old houses, the venerable age-blackened roofs of the cathedral soaring majestically between them. . . .'

According to a 1727 manuscript in the Kem archives, 'the fortress was attacked by Sweden on two occasions, in 7087 [AD 1579] and 7098 [1590]. The churches were burnt down, the dwellings ransacked and most of the people were killed. A few were taken into captivity and a handful managed to escape.' Destruction threatened the whole Suma region, as a report of the Abbot of Solovetsky, written in 1582, makes clear.

In that same year the citadel of Suma was built as a defence against foreign invaders. In the *Kniga Bolshomu Chertezhu* (1627) the citadel is described as an ancient stronghold at the mouth of the Suma river, a hundred and ten *versts* by sea from the Solovetsky monastery. The *Kniga* refers to the close relationship of mutual support which obtained between all the coastal fortresses and fortified settlements under the aegis of the monastery.

The whole fortress-citadel Suma was drastically modernized in 1680 when the old walls were torn down and replaced. The new walls, probably copied from the advanced fortress at Kem, incorporated a double-roofed gallery with embrasures.

By the end of the nineteenth century, however, only one watch-tower, used by the monastery for domestic purposes, remained intact. This octagonal tower was originally the centre-piece of the fortress, dominating the entire area and providing a landmark for maritime traffic. Its front, with wide gates set into it, faced the sea. Above the gates was a little chapel and the whole tower's delicate silhouette recalled the bell-towers of an earlier age.

Another stronghold, north of Suma and Kem, was the fortress town of Kola on the arctic sea-board. The people of Novgorod had been familiar with the Kola peninsula since the eleventh century. The Boyar Republic of Great Novgorod had flourishing trading relations with all the main trading centres of the Baltic, including the Hansa cities, Denmark, and Visby, on the island of Gotland. Among Russian products highly prized by their European trading partners were wax, honey, lard, furs, flax and hemp. The bold and enterprising Novgorodians also ventured far into the Russian north in the pursuit of trade, travelling along the rivers by *ushkui* (a flat-bottomed boat or punt powered by oars and sail), using portage overland when necessary. Life might have been hard and conditions difficult, but traders were drawn on by the vast open spaces and the freedom they enjoyed there. As the Novgorodians explored the north they founded permanent settlements which grew and multiplied. Maritime activity, fishing and trade all increased. Links were forged between the northern region and Moscow by way of the cities of Ustyug, Vologda and Kostroma.

95 Kem. Reconstruction drawing of the tower

96 Kem, on the White Sea. Reconstruction of the massive octagonal corner tower of the town's fortifications, based on still surviving remains; 16th century

The Republic of Great Novgorod fell in 1478 and its lands, including the Kola region, were annexed by Moscow, which now received all the local taxes, in cash and kind, previously due to Novgorod. The year 1532 saw the building of a church on the Kola River, at the site of the ancient settlement of Balitovogorodishche. This was the first church to be built at Murman (now Murmansk) on the Barents Sea. According to Dutch traders who arrived in Murmansk in 1565, Malmus – their name for Kola – consisted of the church and just three houses. One of them belonged to Semyon Vyentsin, who later took monastic vows and assumed the name of Sergey. He built the monastery of St Peter and St Paul in Kola. In 1550 the Kola settlement was granted the title of *ostrog* and a mere thirty years later there were 226 individual households in the town.

The Kola River became a major route for internal and external trade in the middle of the sixteenth century. The town was conveniently situated on the sea-shore, which was navigable throughout the winter, and quickly grew into a large sea-port. The great merchant house of Stroganoff (who were responsible for building many winter settlements), originally of the provincial town of Solvichegodsk, exported their goods via Kola, sending them as far as Dordrecht, Antwerp and Paris. The town teemed with traders from Russia, Holland, Denmark, Norway and many other European countries. It was the starting-point for expeditions to Novaya Zemlya and other islands within the Arctic Circle.

In 1583 a new stronghold was built in Kola by one Maksaka Sudimantov. Teams of carpenters were brought in from neighbouring settlements such as Kerets, Porya Guba, Umba and Kandalaksha, all belonging to the domain of the Solovetsky monastery. The Sudimantov fortress was in a most advantageous position, on a promontory between the mouths of the Kola and Tuloma Rivers, only sixty *versts* from the sea. It was fairly simple, consisting of a stockaded wall and four watch-towers, one at each corner, but proved strong enough to withstand attack by Swedish naval marauders in 1591. Two of the towers were destroyed by fire but the citadel never surrendered. Some ten or fifteen years after its construction the citadel was partly rebuilt and three small towers were added. One of the walls, possibly that facing the sea, was dismantled and replaced by *gorodnya*. Only two of the four original large watch-towers were gated. The new towers and walls had three rows of embrasures.

The fortress was rather densely built up inside the perimeter. The original, small citadel, destroyed in the sixteenth century, was rebuilt. Three of its walls were vertical stockades and the fourth was a horizontal *tarassa*. There were gates in three of its five towers. In addition to this central barbican there were private dwellings and two wooden churches; commercial and government warehouses, storing food and ammunition; a guard-house; and even an open-air prison, which consisted simply of a piece of land surrounded by high, sharpened stockades.

In the seventeenth century the Kola citadel frequently withstood attacks by Scandinavian pirates, its impregnability due to the several rows of fortified walls which surrounded the town. It grew in military strength and significance and within a hundred years was officially listed among the 188 most important stone and wooden fortresses in the land. Kola was rebuilt and strengthened yet again in 1704, at the time of the Northern War. We know that in 1708 there were fifty-nine cannon employed in its defence.

97

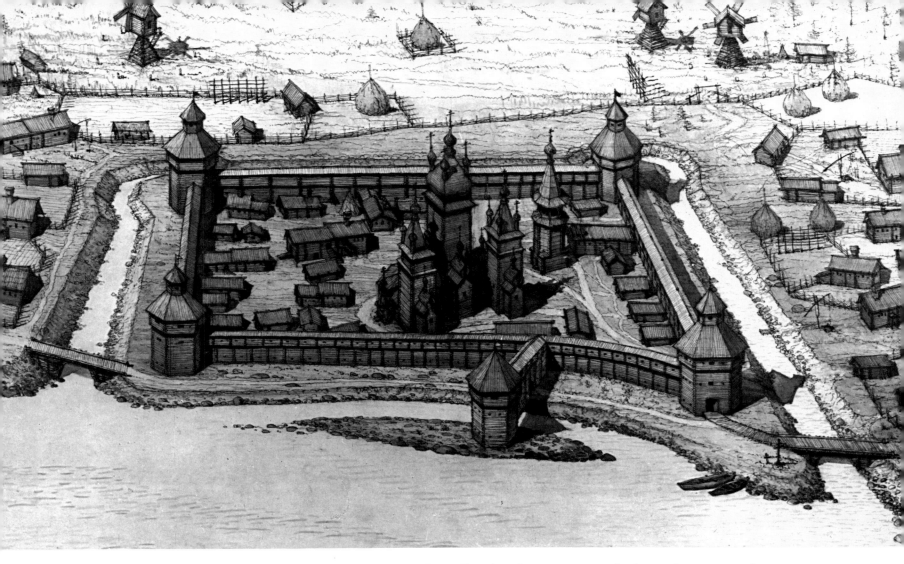

97 The wooden fortress of Kola not far from the present city of Murmansk on the Arctic coast. Reconstruction of its aspect in the 17th century

A number of smaller fortifications were built in the surrounding areas, especially between Kola and the sea. Made of earth and wood, located on high, stony crags, their purpose was to assist in the counter-attack against marauding enemy vessels. The banks of the Kola were protected by massive supporting bulwarks and the rotting walls of the fortress itself were renovated and strengthened by two new hexagonal towers, whose double walls were packed with gravel. The ditch facing the river was rendered even more invulnerable by an *obrub* wall of two hundred logs.

The result of all this activity was a virtually new stronghold by the sea. It still bore the mark of the original design, however, and in this resides the special architectural and historical interest of Kola. The whole development of old wooden fortifications is perfectly illustrated by the changes which took place in this fortress within two hundred years or so. At first there was a simple stockaded settlement; then a small town surrounded by *gorodnya* walls, later replaced by *tarassa* walls with additional stockades; finally, at the beginning of the eighteenth century, it became a mighty stronghold, rendered even more unassailable by improved ramparts, ditches with an *obrub*, and small defence-works on its approaches.

ARCHANGEL

The route from central Russia to the White Sea and the Arctic Ocean followed three major rivers: the Onega, the Northern Dvina and its tributary the Pinega. An official document issued under the authority of Prince Svyatoslav Olgovich, Grand Duke of Kiev, dating from 1137, mentions thirty large settlements on the banks of these rivers. The sparsely populated forest vastnesses around the rivers attracted the princes of Rostov, Suzdal and Moscow as much as the Novgorodians. At the end of the thirteenth century, Prince Andrey Alexandrovich, Grand Duke of Moscow, concluded a treaty with Novgorod whereby the latter promised food and transport to the Grand Duke's representatives going about their business on the White Sea. The town of Kholmogory, on the Dvina, is mentioned for the first time in 1328; the fortress of Orlets was founded in 1342. Both strongholds were built by the Novgorodians in their pursuit of northern trade.

International maritime trade by way of the White Sea, which began at this time, attained a considerable volume within a hundred years, and played an essential role in the financial life of Russia. White Sea ports welcomed trading vessels under the English, Swedish, Dutch, Danish, German, French and even Spanish flags, and there was persistent pressure to increase the number of seaports. In 1583 it thus was decided to build a new fortified harbour on the lower reaches of the Northern Dvina, on the site of a small wooden monastery dedicated to the Archangel Michael. The Tsar charged the governor of the Dvina region to 'build the town without delay and according to the agreed survey and design'. Moscow soon received the message: 'The wooden fortress has been constructed within one year of your command.'

The building programme was not limited to the erection of wooden defences and the construction of the town within. It also included earthworks, enormously labour-intensive because of the ubiquitous swamps and marshes which had to be filled and stabilized. *Obrubi* were placed along the river-banks under the fortress walls to prevent landslides. This castle became the first port of regular, international sea-going trade in Russian history.

The population of New Kholmogory, as the harbour was originally known, grew apace and by the beginning of the seventeenth century there were seven properties belonging to foreign merchants alongside the houses and businesses of many Russian traders. In 1613, to emphasize the significance and independence of this great Russian port, it was rechristened Archangel.

The development of trade and ship-building stimulated the rapid growth of the local economy. Culture and the arts generally began to flourish – architecture above all. Local carpenters, highly experienced in all the subtleties of shipbuilding and the art of ornamentation which went with it, soon proved themselves experts in other fields as well. They had a profound knowledge of all the ways in which wood could be used and an instinctive understanding of line and proportion. Armed with this wisdom they were well placed to create the majestic churches and *izbi* which make up the artistic heritage of the Russian north.

THE ARCTIC REGION

Siberian fortress-building as a branch of Russian architecure begins in 1581 when Yermak and his army crossed the Urals and continued eastwards to the Irtysh River, but Russians had been fascinated by the vast territory beyond the Urals long before. The very earliest chronicles, dating from 1096 to 1114, mention that the Yugra and Samoyed tribes carried on barter with the Novgorodians and describe the abundance of fur in the northern lands. Many half-legendary tales circulated in Russia in the fourteenth century about the mysterious easterners and their strange tongues and a vivid folklore concerning the Siberians persisted for three hundred years or more.

The first Novgorodian expedition to Yugra, under the command of Umbat, took place as early as 1030. Trading links with this remote area during the heyday of the Novgorodian Republic were so extensive that an independent merchant guild, by the name of Yugorshchina, was founded. In the famous chronicle *Povesti vremenykh let* (Chronicle of Times Past), there is an account by Gyurat Rogovich of nomadic tribes inhabiting the Yugra tundra on the coast of the Kara Sea. The *Life of Dimitry Prilutsky* of the fourteenth century describes trade missions to 'pagan peoples, called Yugra, Pechora, Chud and Samoyed'.

The route to Pechora started by the lower reaches of the Mezen river, continued along its tributaries the Peza and the Peza Rochuga, and on by means of portage, to the River Tsilma, which flowed into the Pechora itself, an area famous for its abundance of fish, fur and minerals. Copper ore was discovered in the first half of the fifteenth century; fifty years later deposits of silver were found which, though small, stimulated an intensive search for minerals in the north-eastern region of the country. As the historian N. M. Karamzin wrote in his *History of the Russian State*: 'This discovery gave the Tsar enormous pleasure, and from that moment our people began to mine and smelt metals and mint coins from our own silver.'

Russian trading and industrial settlements began to sprout up along all the routes to Yugra. The most important Muscovite fortress in the Pechora area was Pustozersk, the first town to be built beyond the Arctic Circle, nearly a hundred years earlier than the fortress of Kola.

Ivashka Lastka and his companion Vlastka founded the trade *sloboda* of Ust–Tsilma in 1545, on the right bank of the Pechora river. Some twenty-five years later another *sloboda* sprang up, a hundred *versts* away from Ust–Tsilma, on the river Izhma. The history of these two trading settlements is closely bound up with the development of the Mangazea sea-route, which connected the White Sea coast with the western Siberian rivers. Traders could purchase a large variety of goods at the markets and fairs of Ust–Tsilma, Izhma and Pustozersk and transport them by small boats via the Pechora River and the Pechora Sea to the Kara Sea. They then crossed the Yamal peninsula by portage and continued along the Zelenaya River to the gulf of Ob and finally to the estuary of three Siberian rivers, the Ob, the Pur and the Taz.

This complicated route was in common use by Russian merchants in the fifteenth and sixteenth centuries in spite of the formidable hardships it presented. Foreigners learnt of it from their Russian trading partners and themselves attempted to reach Siberia and even China by way of the Ob. The Russian ambassador to China, Nikolai Spafariy, described this eastward route in a detailed report in the seventeenth century.

The Russian State Treasury suffered severe financial loss as a result of uncontrolled foreign access to Siberia and the consequent unregulated export of fur and fish from the region. To put a stop to this drain of natural resources, and in an attempt to tax it, guards were stationed along the route. One such customs-house was on Matveyevsky Island; another was in the strait between the Barents and Kara Seas; a third was located on the Yamal peninsula.

Such customs and guard-houses were basically fortified dwellings, very similar to the Siberian settlements described earlier in this chapter. The log houses were rather squat, with or without turrets, but always with embrasures in their double walls. The *ostrog* or stockaded town is completely absent, for obvious reasons: then as now, the severe winter, which lasted more than half the year, the permanently frozen ground and the shortage of man-power all discouraged the building of elaborate settlements. There was in any case little need for them, as the posts were only manned during the summer months when the seas and rivers were navigable.

Hunting settlements were also scattered about the polar regions. They were of a somewhat shabby aspect compared with permanent Siberian buildings, being of poor quality logs which had been floated down river. In 1740, two seafarers, F. Minin and D. Sterlegoff, who were carrying out research on the Arctic coast east of the River Yenisey, counted seven hunters' settlements, either inhabited or deserted, between Dikson Island and the mouth of the Pyasina river. They were being lived in by Russian and aboriginal hunters, as well as by non-conformists, outcasts and exiles from all over the country. In other words, the opening up of the far north, not only by official measures but also by the free and independent actions of private individuals, was a very important process both for Russia and for the indigenous population.

EXPLORING THE FAR NORTH

The rapid spread of fishing and trapping activities in the Arctic region stimulated the development of navigation, a very risky and difficult business. Russians had exploited the Arctic for centuries, of course. Walrus had been continuously and intensively hunted by men from Kola and Pustozersk, and sea journeys, possibly between Pechora and Spitsbergen, and between Murmansk and Novaya Zemlya, were commonplace at least as early as the fifteenth century.

One Italian traveller wrote that in the far north 'daylight is almost unknown. All the animals are white, especially the bears.' He was right, more or less, about the fauna (bears, polar foxes and so on) but he was quite mistaken as to the absence of light. The long nights of the polar winter are followed by the equally long summer days. V. F. Zuyev described his journey in 1771 and 1772 along the Arctic coast to the mouth of the Ob as follows: 'The huge sun rolls along the horizon day and night. A man can look at it with his bare eyes for long periods of time without coming to any harm. Its gentle rays soften even the harsh northern landscape. Go, I exhort you, go and see for yourselves.'

Sixteenth-century European geographers had a rather vague picture of the far north which owed more to imagination than to hard fact. They were excited by the possibility of travelling to China by way of the Arctic, and tried to extract information about the far north from Russians in the area. But the latter were familiar with the route only as far as the mouth of the Ob, although it was strongly rumoured that there was indeed a way to get to China via the Arctic ocean. English travellers were proposing a route from the Atlantic to the Pacific via the Arctic. The harsh conditions were a formidable barrier in themselves, but even more crucially, the distribution of land and water beyond the Arctic Circle was simply unknown. These optimists could only hope, like Magellan, to find the channel which would eventually lead them to China and India. English and Dutch expeditions, however, met with no success throughout the sixteenth century, and there was general pessimism as to the possibility of discovering a north-eastern passage to the Orient. I. Massa, a Dutch geographer who lived in Moscow for some years, wrote in 1608: 'I now know, and can prove, that there is no northern sea route to China. All those who persist in this endeavour are doomed to disappointment.' Time and the efforts of Russian seamen and Siberian explorers gradually proved him wrong.

They discovered new estuaries and islands and made the first surveys and maps of the Arctic coast of the Asian mainland. They defied hardship and death in their struggle to open the way for the next generation to realize the ancient dream. Strong winds forced their boats back to the shore and massive ice-floes often trapped and crushed their flimsy hulls. Even thin ice could damage the sides of vessels buffeted by capricious winds. Boats were frequently frozen where they lay and the sailors forced to walk across the treacherous ice until they reached land. But by the seventeenth century the battle had been largely won, and the whole region had begun to be comprehensively surveyed by Russian explorers.

ARCTIC FORTIFIED SETTLEMENTS

Let us now turn to the fortresses of arctic Siberia. The oldest of these fortified towns was Obdorsk, renamed Salekhard in 1933. The original name derives from the river Ob and the word *dor*, meaning 'place' in the language of the local Komi tribe. Salekhard derives from the tongue of another local tribe, the Samoyeds (or Nentsi): *sale* means village and *khard* means promontory. Russian arrivals called their fortress by yet another name, Nosovoi Gorodok (or Cape Town).

In 1592 Tsar Fedor Ivanovich dispatched a battalion of Cossacks to make a study of the northern Ob area and to integrate it into the mainstream of Russian life. Reaching an old *ostrog* on the river Lyapin, already colonized by troops under Prince S. Kurbskiy a hundred years earlier, the battalion split into several groups which went their separate ways. The following year six new fortresses were built: 100–02 Yuilsk, Berezov, Kazym, Sartynino, Kodsk and Obdorsk itself.

Obdorsk was constructed under the command of the governor, Nikifor Trakhaniotov. By 1595 it had grown into a small stockaded town inhabited only in the summer months of June, July and August. Some hundred years later the wooden fortifications of the town were renovated by order of Empress Anna

113

Ioanovna and a unit of Cossacks was permanently installed to protect the fortress against attack by hostile nomadic tribes all year round. The unit numbered fifty to begin with, and later doubled in size but by the end of the eighteenth century they were no longer needed; the native tribes had been subdued, the bloody conflicts over.

Obdorsk was the most northerly fortified position on the Lower Ob river. Further up, towards the Kara Sea, the only signs of human habitation were the occasional tents of the nomadic Ostyak (or Khanti) and Samoyed tribes and a few nondescript dwellings belonging to Russian merchants.

So it was that, in the second half of the sixteenth century, Muscovy strode confidently beyond the Urals. This whole vast area, stretching eastwards from the Ob estuary, and famous among hunters and traders for its abundant supply of fur, and the town of the same name, were known to the Russians as Mangazea, or Molgonzea, a name derived from a local Samoyed tribe. The authorities in Moscow were unwilling to tolerate uncontrolled exploitation of the region and in 1600 Boris Godunov sent a large expedition, under the command of Prince Miron Shchakhovsky and the *strelets* major Danila Khripunov, to return Mangazea to the authority of the state. The expedition was put together rather hurriedly and the boats proved unsuitable for the sea journey. The troops were forced to trudge hundreds of miles over the tundra and were finally destroyed by the combined attacks of Samoyed warriors and rebellious Russian merchants and traders.

The following year yet another expedition set out for Mangazea. It was twice the size of the previous unit, consisting of two hundred well equipped soldiers commanded by Prince Vasily Mosalsky and Savluk Pushkin, a boyar. By order of **98** Boris Godunov they founded the town of Mangazea on the site of an existing trading-post by the river Taz. At the time, it was the most northern as well as the most eastern town in Russian Siberia, and the administrative centre of the new territory. It consisted of a wooden fortress with some twenty houses providing year-round quarters for the growing *strelets* garrison, and further accommodation for customs officers and tax collectors. There were also permanent mobile patrols round the settlement: there should be nowhere to hide from the implacable eye of authority. And yet we know from various urgent messages reaching Moscow from local governors that the rebellious people of Mangazea refused to bow to the new administration and violated its rigid regulations at every turn.

The social mix of the town was rich: the majority were seamen, traders and merchants who had come from the White Sea coast of northern Russia. In addition there were many people who had left Russia and arrived in Mangazea in search of freedom and prosperity. 'Fugitives from Mezen and Pustozersk turn up in Mangazea', reported Governor Dimitry Pogozhev to Moscow, 'together with tax-evaders, debtors, robbers and other criminals.'

A directive (*ukaz*) from Moscow in the year 1619 forbade travel to Mangazea via the Kara Sea and portage over the Yamal peninsula. This left only one route, that overland by way of Tobolsk and Berezov. The reasoning behind this *ukaz* was that unofficial trading by Russians with foreign merchants was depriving the State Treasury of vital revenue. Cargo boats continuously plied between Pechora and 'the second Baghdad', as Mangazea was warmly referred to at the beginning of the seventeenth century, so the closure of the sea route between the two towns

98   Imaginative reconstruction of the fortress of Mangazea on the River Taz (whose estuary joins that of the Ob). Founded at the beginning of the 17th century, it was then both the northernmost and the easternmost settlement in Siberia. Finally abandoned after a disastrous fire in 1643

99   New Mangazea (now Turukhansk) was established on the lower Yenisey in 1672, 29 years after the destruction of Old Mangazea. The engraving dates from the 17th century

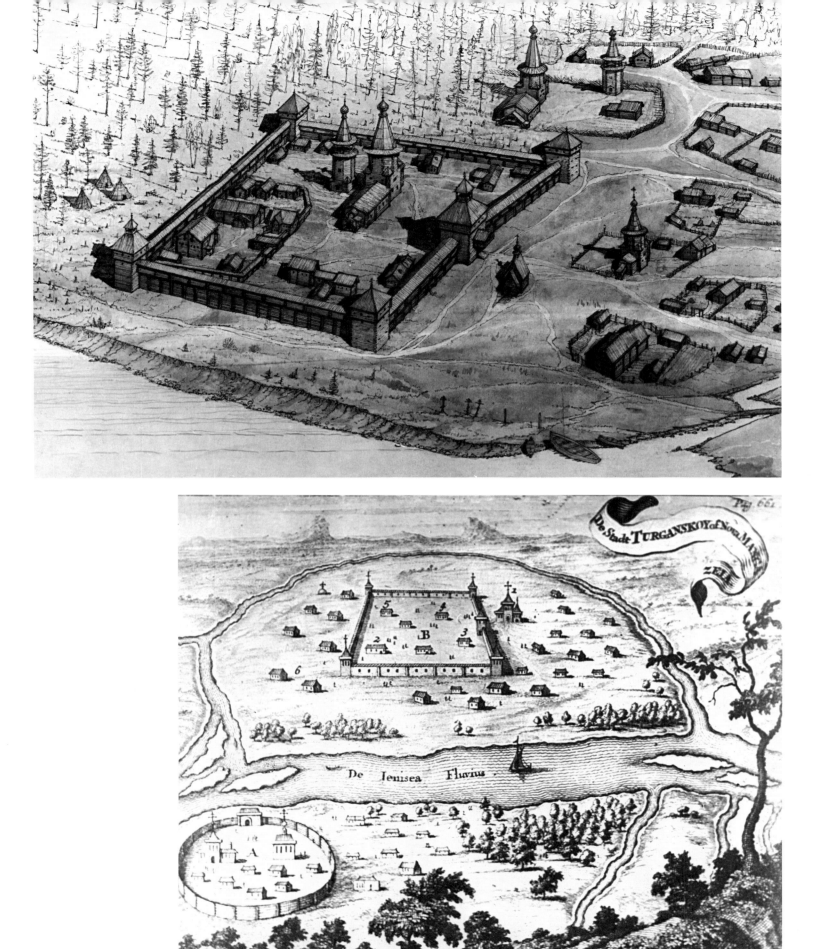

De Stadt TURGANSKOY of Nova MANGZEE

De Ienisea Fluvius

100   The Yuilsk *ostrog* was established as a customs post on the River Kazym (an eastern tributary of the Ob, seen here) at the end of the 16th century; it is a long since abandoned, uninhabited site

99

100–02

seriously undermined the prosperity of the Pechora settlements. After 1619 the *sloboda* of Ust–Tsilma, the *ostrog* of Pustozersk and the town of Mangazea itself fell into decay. The polar fox population also diminished because of indiscriminate over-hunting; and the final blow was the total destruction of Mangazea by fire in 1643. The town was deserted by its inhabitants and never rebuilt. Twenty-nine years later New Mangazea (today Turukhansk) was founded on the site of the Turukhansk winter settlement, on the River Yenisey.

Revenue from duties levied by customs and excise amounted to thirty per cent of the gross value of all goods imported into and exported from Siberia and was therefore an important source of income for the state, close attention being paid to its collection. The government in Moscow repeatedly ordered Siberian governors to establish customs-houses on all major routes. The first known Russian *ostrog* in Siberia is mentioned in a chronicle of 1445, and one such post grew into the fortress of Yuilsk. It was built at the end of the sixteenth century in the dense and marshy taiga on the River Kazym, a tributary of the Ob. Almost nothing of the *ostrog* now remains but it was a typical example of a small Siberian fortress, possessing only two towers. Yuilsk stood on a very important thoroughfare connecting the upper reaches of the Kazym river with the town of Berezov, itself on the Ob. As tradition dictated, it was at the conjunction of two rivers, near an ancient camp of the Ostyak nomads. Its main, northern tower monitored access to the town from the road; the smaller, southern tower surveyed the river. They were surrounded by a vertical stockade 3.6 metres high, in the form of a trapezium whose asymmetry probably indicates an early date; later stockades were usually rectangular in design. The total length of the walls was 180 metres. There was one peculiarity in their construction: each log had a vertical groove on one side into which its neighbour fitted, recalling a design common in Russia (excluding the Kiev *Rus*) in former days. The stockade was additionally strengthened from the inside by long horizontal struts 20×10 centimetres thick.

101 Yuilsk *ostrog*: reconstruction of the
gate-tower, stockade and associated
buildings

102 Yuilsk *ostrog*: remains of the south
tower found on the site of the
fortification

Tobolsk, Siberia, in an engraving by Georg Adam Schliessing of 1694 (from *Derer bey den Czaaren in Russland*)

103   Tobolsk, Siberia, in an engraving by Georg Adam Schliessing of 1694 (from *Derer bey den Czaaren in Russland*)

104   Tobolsk on the Irtysh (a major tributary of the Ob) was an important fortified settlement on the overland route to the Mangazeas. 17th-century plan

A secondary function of this *ostrog* was the collection of taxes from the Samoyeds, mainly paid in furs. Local geography was such that it was impossible to pass the fortress unnoticed. The only safe way to travel was by river. In summer the marshes were treacherous but the river was navigable. In winter the icy, impenetrable forest and dangerous animals threatened the lonely traveller with the risk of getting lost in the seemingly endless winter night, but the frozen river was familiar and sure.

In the last quarter of the sixteenth century the river Tura became the main artery for travel to Siberia. In 1586 the town of Tyumen sprang up, followed by Verkhoturye (1598) and Turinsk (1600), all three along the banks of the Tura. Tobolsk, soon to become the principal city of Siberia, was built in 1587, where the River Tobol meets the Irtysh. Berezov (1593), Surgut (1594) and Obdorsk (1595) were built on the mighty Ob; and finally, of course, Mangazea, on the river Taz in 1601.

103, 104

The same period saw the first mass immigration of peasants into Siberia and within a hundred years they made up forty-four per cent of its Russian population. The Irtysh and its tributaries became the main route for these people.

105 Krasnoyarsk on the upper Yenisey, among the southernmost of the Siberian fortified settlements. Reconstructed section of a gate-tower with plan and scales in *sazhen*

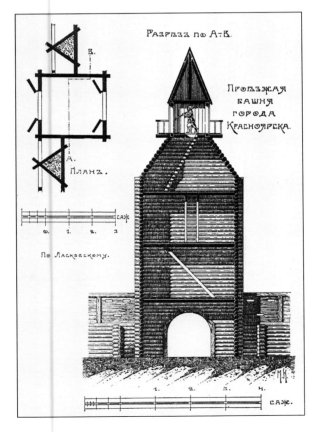

EASTERN SIBERIA

The exploration of eastern Siberia began in the first quarter of the seventeenth century. Soldiers and merchants were in the vanguard of this daring project, among them Vasily Poyarkov, the discoverer of the Amur river. They were often accompanied by local guides, Evenks, Yakuts, Buryats, Yukagirs and Chukchis, for example, who helped the newcomers to find convenient routes and make friendly contacts with the natives. The pioneers crossed the Yenisey and continued eastwards along its tributaries, the Nizhnaya (Lower) Tunguska, the Podkamenaya (Stony) and the Verkhnyaya (Upper) Tunguska, constructing winter settlements as they went. The largest and most important was the Krasnoyarsk *ostrog*, for many years the southernmost fortress in Siberia. A whole system of smaller fortresses and fortified winter settlements grew up round it.

East of the Yenisey the Russians built their first settlements on the Upper Lena river. In 1630 *sotnik* (a Cossack lieutenant) Ivan Galkin built the winter settlement of Ilim and renovated another, constructed only a year earlier near the Kuta estuary. The fortress of Chechuisk was built two or three years later, on the portage route between the Lower Tunguska and the Lena. The most significant event in the exploration of the Lena basin was the building of an *ostrog* at Yakutsk.

The next step was to move up the Lena river, south towards Lake Baikal. Six major expeditions explored the area between 1627 and 1661, building fourteen large *ostrogi* in the process. In 1627, for example, Maxim Perfilyev, a Cossack chieftain, built the fortress of Angarsk near the Shaman Stone, forty kilometres from the modern city of Irkutsk. The Ust-Ilimsk fortress was constructed a year later at the mouth of the Ilim, followed by Bratsk (1630–35) and Upper Angarsk (1647), both on the Angara river, and Barguzinsk (1649), east of Lake Baikal.

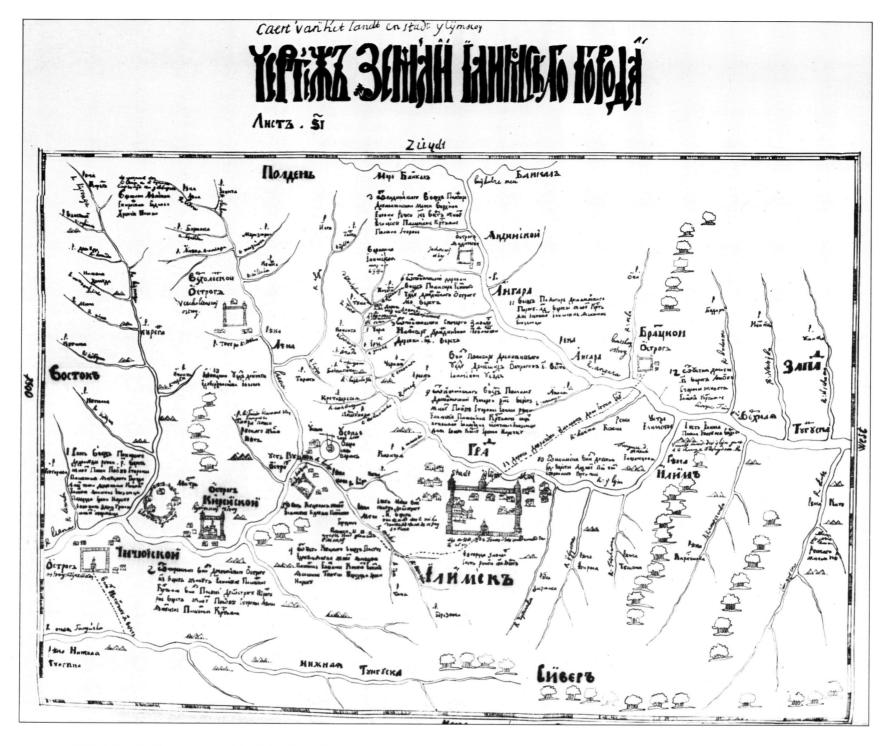

106 Map (without any scale) of Ilimsk and
surroundings at the end of the 17th century, by
S. Remezov. The map faces south, not north, and even
shows, at the top, the River Angara emerging from
Lake Baikal

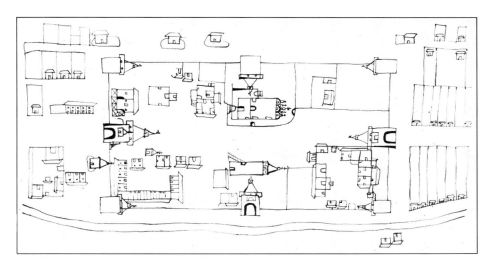

107 Plan of Ilimsk in 1703, showing the eight towers on its surrounding ramparts and its church and belfry, besides many houses

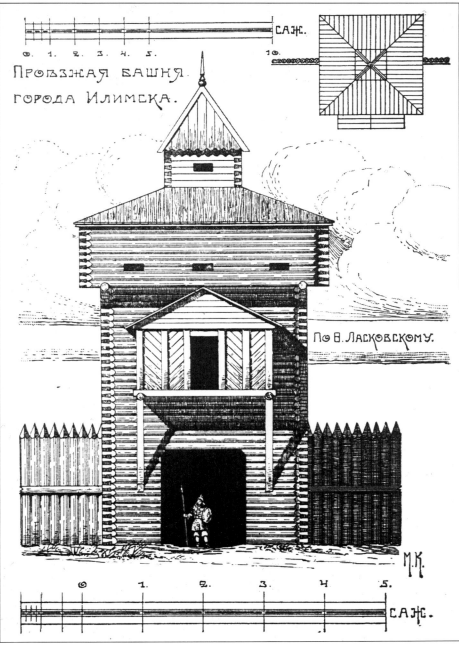

ПРОѢЗЖАЯ БАШНЯ.
ГОРОДА ИЛИМСКА.

По В. ЛАСКОВСКОМУ.

108 Surviving tower at Ilimsk, a major strong point on the route eastward to the Lena basin, dating from 1647

109 Ilimsk. Reconstruction of gate-tower (scale in *sazhen*)

By this time there was a recognizable style common to all Siberian fortresses, in spite of the differing demands, conditions and environments with which they had to contend. Take, for example, the fortress of Ilimsk. This town grew on the site of a winter settlement founded in 1631, on the main route connecting the Ilim and Lena rivers. It soon became the most important strong-point between Yeniseysk and Yakutsk. In 1647 a new *ostrog* was built by Grigory Demyanov on the site of the old winter settlement. At first it was rather small, consisting, like Yuilsk, of two towers surrounded by a stockade, except that there was a gate in only one of the towers. Its main task was to mount surveillance over the river. Nineteen years later a new, much larger *ostrog* was built, one and a half kilometres from the old one, on the high right bank of the river.

This *ostrog* is well described in Remezov's *Chertezhnaya Kniga Sibiri*. It is several times larger than any of its neighbours: there were eight turreted towers in an oblong stockade. Three of them, the Holy Saviour (seventeen metres high and the only surviving remnant of the whole fortress), the Presentation of the Virgin and the Epiphany, were gated. Inside the stockade stood the five-domed Church of the Holy Saviour, with next to it an octagonal bell-tower of thirty-two metres under a 'tent' roof. Nearby were official buildings, including the governor's quarters. There were also government store-houses, an inn with twenty beds, guard-houses and barracks for the garrison. All the buildings were carefully placed according to old Russian building regulations which stipulated a distance of at least nine metres between each, a requirement increased to sixty-three metres by Peter the Great in 1722 as a fire precaution. Two peasant settlements sprang up round the fortress and, as the land was extremely fertile, Ilimsk became the granary as well as the administrative centre of all eastern Siberia.

The fortress of Bratsk, also described by Remezov, is a sixth the size of Ilimsk. It was built, as usual, at the conjunction of two rivers, the Angara and the Oka. Its walls had four towers, two of which still survive. (One is on display at the open-air museum of Kolomenskoe near Moscow, the other in the Angara Villages Museum. They had to be removed because of the construction of a reservoir some years ago.) These particular towers, unturreted, were on two floors, each with its independent entrance. There was a trap-door in the ceiling between the floors. The interior of the tower now in Kolomenskoe has been restored to its original state. It is a small, traditional *kurnaya izba* with a smoke-hole in the wall above the stove. There are three small windows set low in the wall opposite the door, the middle one slightly higher than its fellows, a common feature of log houses and churches. The Bratsk fortress soon lost its military importance and developed into a prosperous farming settlement, its inhabitants earning additional revenue from fishing and hunting. They were also cargo carriers, transporting tea, for example, from Irkutsk via the Angara river to Yeniseysk. It was this economic development which confirmed earlier military successes and persuaded local tribes to accept the agricultural way of life led by the Russian peasantry. This process assimilated the region into the Russian homeland.

In 1652 Yakov Pokhabov, with a small detachment of Cossacks, reached the source of the Angara, Lake Baikal. Nine years later the Irkutsk *ostrog* was built on the high bank of the Angara, opposite the mouth of its tributary, the Irkut. It was surrounded by a ditch and a wall with three towers.

110   Bratsk: a surviving tower of the minor fortification south-west of Ilimsk (it has been moved elsewhere because of flooding for the Bratsk hydro-electric scheme)

111 (*above left*) Upper floor of the Bratsk tower

112 Detail of entry to the Bratsk tower

113 Bratsk. Side view of the surviving tower

114 Bratsk: reconstructed tower elevations viewed from outside (above) and inside (scales in *sazhen*)

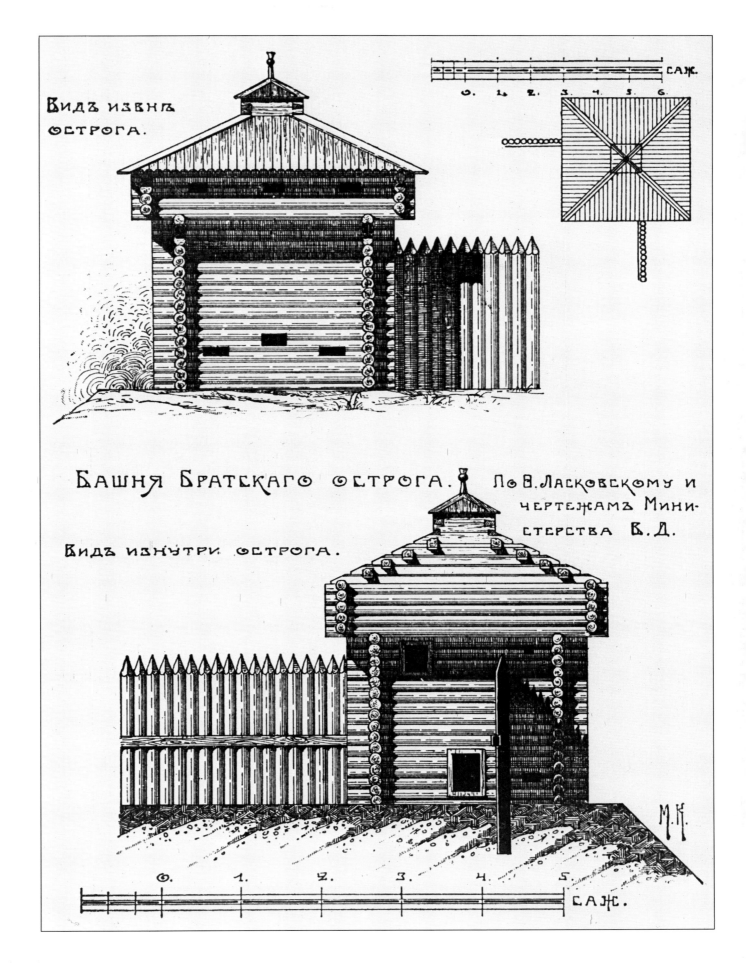

ВИДЪ ИЗВНѢ ОСТРОГА.

БАШНЯ БРАТСКАГО ОСТРОГА. По В. Ласковскому и чертежамъ Министерства В. Д.

ВИДЪ ИЗНУТРИ ОСТРОГА.

САЖ.

0. 1. 2. 3. 4. 5. 6.

0. 1. 2. 3. 4. 5.

САЖ.

М. К.

Four towers and a church stood inside the stockade. The ground floors, as in all Siberian towers, were used as living accommodation and for general household purposes. In Irkutsk, for example, they were lived in by unmarried Cossacks. A contemporary account describes the fortress as follows: 'Irkutsk, on the left bank of the Angara, presents an impressive view. There are forty or so peasant and Cossack dwellings built round the Church of the Holy Saviour. The land is very rich. Many native tribes, such as the Brati, Tungusi etc. live there and pay tribute to the Russian Tsar. Only the men pay this tribute, a levy of two polar fox furs each.'

Irkutsk found itself at the crossroads of trade routes between Europe and the Orient and its economy developed accordingly. In 1764 the city, with thirty thousand inhabitants, became the administrative centre of the province. The modern city of Irkutsk has all but obliterated the old town and it is almost impossible to imagine its appearance in earlier days.

The nearby village of Belskaya, however, gives us an authentic picture of a rural Siberian fortress. It stands near the site of the former fortress of Belsk, on the hilly bank of the River Belaya (the White River), a tributary of the Angara. The fortress was founded in 1691 to defend the area against Mongol incursions. Only 116–18 one tall watch-tower has survived, 4.1 metres square. It is on two floors, with a turret. The logs which make up its base are up to 35 centimetres in diameter. There are three rows of embrasures, one under the roof and the other two on the ground floor. We may deduce from the position of the embrasures, on the southern as well as the eastern sides, that this was a corner tower, and the lie of the land supports this supposition. The hill on which it stands descends almost vertically: it may be an artificial earthwork surrounded by a moat, as in nearby Irkutsk. The tower is supported from the outside by huge wooden piles, although its base rests directly on the ground.

The finest flowering of Siberian defence architecture was undoubtedly the fortress of Yakutsk, one of the largest in the country and the capital of eastern Siberia. It consisted of several churches, many administrative buildings, workshops and houses, and was protected by two mighty walls, separated from each other at a distance equal to the range of a bullet. The inner wall was topped by a low-pitched, double-sloping roof overhanging a gallery on both sides. One gallery facing into the citadel was left open; the other, looking over the outer wall, was 121 enclosed. Each city wall was further strengthened by eight multi-storey towers, four at the corners and four in between. In the seventeenth century the walls fell 119, 120, 122 into decay and, of the whole defence system, only one gated tower survives.

Yakutsk became the main staging-post in the vast territory between Moscow and the Pacific Ocean. For two hundred years it was the starting-point for numerous scientific expeditions studying the Arctic and Pacific coasts of north-eastern Siberia. Furs, skins, walrus tusks and other valuable goods from areas as far apart as the Aleutian Islands, Kolyma and Alaska were collected here for transportation to Europe.

About twenty smaller fortresses and winter settlements grew up around Yakutsk. The most important to the west were Chechuisk, Olekmensk, Charinsk, Ust–Potomsk, Upper, Middle and Lower Vilyusk; to the east: Okhotsk and Ust–Maisk. North and far to the north-east of Yakutsk were Olensk, Zhigansk, Verkhoyansk, Nizhneyansk, Zashiversk, Podshchiversk, Uyandinsk, Alazeysk, Anadirsk, Chendonst, and Upper, Middle and Lower Kolymsk.

115 The *ostrog* of Irkutsk, far to the south of Ilimsk and Bratsk, was founded in 1661. The reconstruction by B. Lebedinsky shows how this fort stood beside the River Angara, some way below the point where it flows out of Lake Baikal

116 Belsk, near Irkutsk, photographed about the beginning of the 20th century. It was the site of a minor fort

117　Belsk more recently, its restored log-tower
contrasting with the whitewashed brick of the church

118　The rare surviving tower from the Belsk fort

119 Yakutsk, the gate-tower before restoration

120 Yakutsk. View looking upwards into the pyramidal roof of the gate-tower, to show the log construction

121 Yakutsk, now as in the past, the metropolis of north-eastern Siberia. The drawing by V. G. Korolenko, made at the end of the 19th century, shows how much then remained of the ancient *ostrog*

122 Yakutsk. The one surviving gate-tower, carefully restored, is here seen against the background of blocks of flats

Якутскій городок. Остатки казацкихъ укрепленій. Съ рисунка В. Г. Королен

Зашиверскъ

123 Zashiversk. One of the latest drawings (1820) of the ill-fated small town

124 Zashiversk (established 1639). This empty landscape on the Indigirka, remote and inaccessible even by Siberian standards, recalls the tragedy of this settlement, wiped out for good by smallpox in the 1820s. The church, just visible here, still stands (see 234–5)

125 Zashiversk in an engraving of 1784

126 Reconstruction of the Zashiversk *ostrog* as it might have appeared early in the 18th century. The Indigirka is shown choked with floating ice in the spring thaw (probably June, in that area)

127 Reconstruction – based on scanty evidence – of the *ostrog* on the Alazeya

128 The Alazeysk *ostrog* stood here, as proved by some decaying logs and floor-boards. From here the next river system (of the Kolyma) was explored

129 Fortress on the Maly Anyui – a tributary of the Kolyma – not far from the Bering Straits. This fort, some six thousand kilometres from Moscow, and dating from the 1840s, was probably the last timber stronghold ever built in the Russian empire. The historic winter photograph (1896) shows sledges and dogs outside the walls

130 The same fortress. External walls; the zigzag ground plan; internal walls with raised walk for the defenders

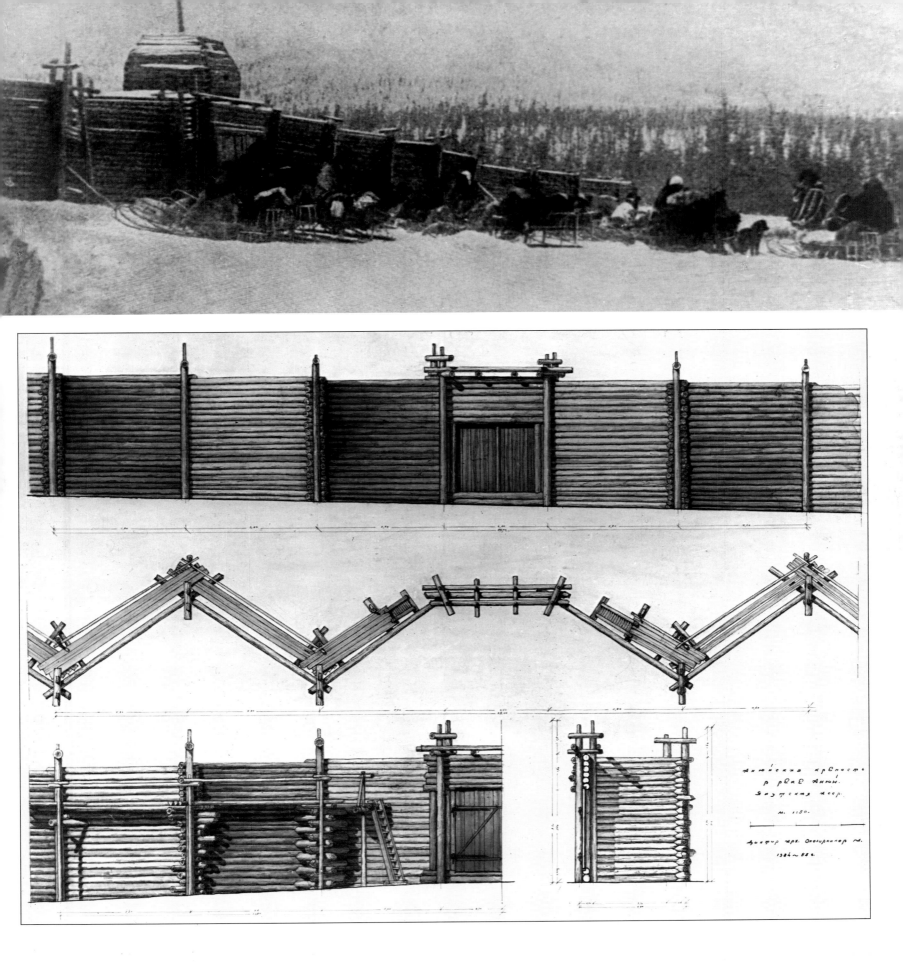

After the construction of the Yakutsk fortress in 1632, Russian colonists began to explore and settle the outlying regions of Siberia. The movement towards the north-east was unorganized and spontaneous, although it coincided strongly with the interests of the state, which forwent petty administrative controls and encouraged initiative and creativity on the part of the new population. As a result, overland and water routes were established connecting Yakutsk with the rivers Yana, Indigirka, Alazeya and Kolyma. Travellers would often get to their destination by water and return overland, or vice versa. Selivanko Kharitonov led the first expedition to reach the Indigirka from Yakutsk via the River Yana and the Taihayanas mountain range. In 1640 he broke through to Kolyma by sea. Ivan Rebrov, a Cossack from Tobolsk, discovered the sea route to the Yana and the Indigirka. Several winter settlements were built along these rivers, among them Verkhoyansk (1638) and Zashiversk (1639), which grew into important towns. The days of Zashiversk were numbered, however: it was ravaged by smallpox in the 1820s and its population wiped out. Its buildings rotted and decayed and apart from the church only a few marshy mounds now remain.

123–6 Zashiversk's impregnable fortress was hidden between the Verkhoyansk and Stanovoy ranges, connected to Yakutsk and Kolyma by a long and dangerous route, known in the eighteenth century as the Kolymsky *trakt*. I. Khudyakov, a political exile, wrote that travelling along the *trakt* was crueller than all the exigencies of hard labour itself. The fortress was situated on the river, protected by the mountains from the icy arctic winds. Its complement of store-houses, dwellings, shops, moorings, defensive walls and towers, churches and bell-towers created a picturesque urban landscape familiar to the immigrants from the European Russian north. A few nomads' tents scattered outside the walls might remind them that their true homes lay far away to the west. Three or four weeks

127 away by boat and on foot was the Alazeya with its own fortress, Alazeysk, the centre for the exploration of Kolyma. It was conveniently located at the conjunction of the Alazeya and the Buor–Yuryakh rivers, a location which gave it additional protection against aggressive nomads. It never fulfilled its primary function, however, as the Russian Cossacks quickly made friendly contact with the native tribes and even intermarried with them. Only a few logs of the fortress

128 survive but even these pitiable remains bespeak a mighty stronghold. Where did the builders find these great logs, half a metre in diameter, in an area so poor in flora that a tree would not exceed ten to fifteen centimetres even after a hundred years?

The journey over the plain to Kolyma from Alazeysk took a good ten days by trail. The Russian pioneers first settled in Middle and Lower Kolymsk and then moved up to Upper Kolymsk. The villages along this river attracted more Russian settlers than any other area in Yakutia; by 1850 there were a thousand people living in the Kolyma district alone, compared with seven hundred living along the Anabara, Olenka, Yana and Indigirka. By the middle of the seventeenth century the bulk of arctic Siberia had been explored and settled. The huge territory, divided by marshes, mountain ranges and great rivers, was united by an elaborate network of tracks, with many fortresses and winter settlements at their junctions. Sea routes connected estuaries one to another. Russians found the Great Northern Seaway round the Siberian continent in spite of storms, ice and the scepticism of foreigners.

COLOUR PLATE

XIII   Surviving tower from the 17th-century wooden fortifications of Bratsk, Irkutsk Province, Siberia

XIII

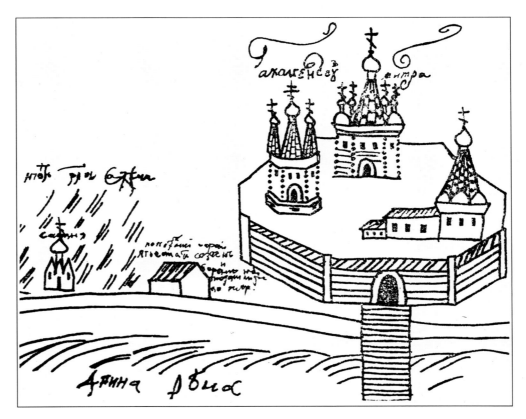

131　The fortified monastery of St Michael the Archangel (after which the city of Archangel on the White Sea was named). A 17th-century drawing

Fortresses inside the Arctic Circle – there were only about ten of them – were quite different from those in European Russia and central Siberia. Firstly, they were much smaller and secondly, their defensive requirements were modest because of the primitive weaponry of the enemy. Their walls and towers were more for purposes of demarcation than of protection. A typical example was the little wooden fortress of Anyuisk on the river Maly Anyui, a tributary of the Kolyma. It was the last defensive structure to be built in Siberia, and dates from the 1840s. Constructed of slim larch logs, it had turreted gates and, inside the walls, a small chapel, a guard-house and about a dozen shabby dwellings. Nomad encampments surrounded the settlement and the howling of a hundred huskies could be heard from inside the stockade. A photograph taken in 1896 gives us an idea of two elements of the fortress, the wall and the tower. The latter recalls the store-house tower of Ponomarev; the polygonal wall, of horizontal interlocking logs, distinguishes the little fortress from most other defensive structures, though it resembles the fences round monasteries and *pogosti*.

129

130

COLOUR PLATE

XIV　Gate tower (*nadvratnaya bashnya*) from the monastery of St Nicholas Korelsky near Archangel; late 17th century. Now re-erected in the open-air museum at Kolomenskoe, Moscow

FORTIFIED MONASTERIES

Monasteries and fortresses had one important function in common in these outposts of the empire, namely to represent the official policy of uniting the far-

132   Gate-tower and walls of the
St Nicholas Korelsky Monastery by the
Northern Dvina estuary near Archangel.
A bleak winter scene photographed
about 1900

133   The arched passage through the
same gate-tower as re-erected at
Kolomenskoe, Moscow (compare
plate XIV)

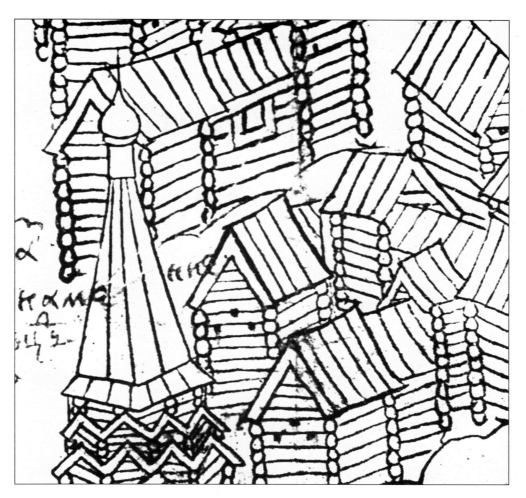

134 Part of the monastery dedicated to Our Lady of Tikhvin (a well-known icon). The sketch was by Ivan Zelenin, 1679

flung territories under the authority of Moscow. One of the oldest northern Russian monasteries, recorded as early as the end of the fourteenth century, was that of St Nicholas in Chukhchenemsk, eight *versts* east of Kholmogory. Two

131 other monasteries, St Michael the Archangel and St Nicholas Korelsky, were built on the estuary of the Northern Dvina at the same time. The first written record of

132 St Nicholas occurs in 1419. According to legend, a wooden church of St Nicholas stood on the site, over the bodies of two drowned brothers, Antony and Felix. It was founded at the wish of their grieving mother, Marfa Boretskaya, the governor of Novgorod. The monastery was rebuilt several times in the course of more than five hundred years. In 1667 and 1674 two stone churches were erected there and in 1691 and 1692 a six-tower stockade enclosed the monastery. In 1880 this stockade, by then partly rotted, was renovated and encased with the flat and featureless timbers so fashionable in the last century. In 1932 the main gated

XIV tower was transferred to the Kolomenskoe Museum where it was restored by the architect P. D. Baranovski, who also partly recreated the vanished stockade. The

133 tower evokes a sacred rather than a secular mood: it is an octagon resting on a rectangle, faithful to the principle on which most wooden churches and bell-towers were built in old Russia. Such church and monastery towers exude a gentle lyricism in contrast with the menacing sense of invulnerability transmitted by the great Siberian strongholds, and it is to sacred buildings that we turn in the next chapter.

4 · Churches

Fires engulf the heavens with their all-consuming fires
Choirs glorify the timeless moment, angels' choirs
'Why hast thou forsaken me, O my Father, why?
'Mother, Mother, weep not, when I die.'

Anna Akhmatova

THE bells rang out their clamorous message . . . festive, solemn or sorrowful, demanding, alarming, anxious, calling the congregation to prayer, weddings and funerals, warning of fire and flood and reporting every catastrophe. They angrily announced the enemy's approach and when victory was won, sang the bravery of the motherland's defenders and mourned her dead heroes.

The bells of Russia's wooden churches are dumb now but the pages of her history, imbued with the thoughts and feelings of her people, rustle on in the silent churches, chapels and memorial crosses which record the story of the past. Ancient wooden churches are the finest achievement of Russian architecture. Dozens have fallen victim to time, fire, snow and rain, and to the well-meant or destructive attentions of men. But churches, bell-towers and chapels do survive, mainly in remote northern areas, on the steep banks of lakes and rivers, in valleys, forests and plains. They have been abandoned long since, even by parishioners in their Sunday best on high days and holidays, but a new breed of admirers is rediscovering them, coming from far and wide to drink from the wells of ancient wisdom.

THE POGOST

135 South-western view of the chapel at Fedorovskaya on the River Onega. It was later transferred to the Maliye Korely open-air museum at Archangel, headquarters of the Province (see 147)

The word *pogost* had many meanings. Ancient chronicles describe the *pogost* as the principal village of a large district. For census purposes it was any settlement, however small, with a church. Usually, the name of a *pogost* consisted of its church and settlement; sometimes a nearby river, lake or town was included.

136 (left, above) Cemetery in Yakutia

137 (left) Woodland cemetery, Priangarye district of Irkutsk Province, Siberia

138 (above) Old wooden crosses from graves in Karelia. The inner crosses, carved in relief, are of the usual Russian Orthodox pattern with two cross-bars at the top and an oblique bar near the foot; to left and right the spear and rod with sponge. The lettering on these and most Russian crosses is partly Byzantine-influenced. At the top: 'Tsar Slavy' (King of Glory). Above the arms: 'IC XC' (first and last letters of 'Jesus Christ' in Greek or Slavonic). Below the arms: 'NIKA' (Victory, from Greek)

139   Shuyeretskoe, Karelia. Roofed
crosses in an ancient graveyard

140   Varzuga on the Kola Peninsula.
Graves among the dunes

16–20

139

For example, a review of Onega *pogosti* carried out in 1582–83 by a Moscow official, Andrey Plesheyev, mentions 'the Spasky [Saviour] *pogost* in Kizhi by Lake Onega'. Another example is the *pogost* of Pochozero, formerly the busy centre of a large district, now reduced to a dozen buildings. It still has two churches and a bell-tower and its full title was Philippovsky–Pochozersky *pogost*.

Nowadays a *pogost* simply denotes a country cemetery. Wandering among the young trees, meadows and fields surrounding a village, you may well come across ancient groves of fir and pine. Their dark but gentle outline, standing out against the landscape, shelters the cemetery.

People are never more conservative than when they bury their dead. Generations of Russian peasants honoured the graves of their loved ones in an unchanging tradition which ceased only at the beginning of our century. The memorials they built over those graves express their sense of poetry and beauty. Old burial grounds are now extremely rare, though even ten or twenty years ago they were still common in a few virtually uninhabited and isolated northern areas of the country. Some remarkable examples are to be seen in the villages of Kovda and Shuyeretskoe on the White Sea, in the Karelian hamlet of Ust–Yandoma, in the *pogost* of St Ilya (Elijah the Prophet) on Lake Vodlozero and in remote parts of Siberia.

These ancient cemeteries – apart from those in the Yakutia region of Siberia – adhered to the rite of the Old Believers. Their characteristic grave memorials are the *domovina* and the *stolbets*. The *domovina* was an oblong rectangle under a tiny, double-sloping roof of horizontal or vertical boards. It was built from logs (the older and rarer ones) or plain boards. The *domovina*, whose size varied with the sex and age of the deceased, was placed directly onto the grave-mound and served to decorate the grave and to protect it from damage. More importantly, perhaps, it symbolized the Old Believers' conviction that the spirit of the deceased lived on in the *domovina* itself; the word derived from *dom* (house) and was a miniature version of a simple *izba* with a *brus* type plan. Its roof was complete with *shelom* and *prichelini* (the latter with carved suns and other symbols originating in pagan times).

There was a tiny window in the west wall for communicating with the soul of the departed, so tiny that an adult hand could hardly squeeze through. The window was cut according to a number of traditional designs, circular, semi-circular, square, oblong and rhomboid. On special days relatives would place little presents in the *domovina* for the loved one: wool, colourful material, needles and thread for women, hunting and fishing equipment for men. Toys were left for children, and food and small coins for all the dead. Such gifts were sacrosanct, safe from even the most cynical and hard-bitten criminal.

The *stolbets* (from *stolb*, a column) was placed at the head of the grave, close up to the eastern wall of the *domovina*. This little, roofed column, square, round or octagonal, measured from 70 to 180 centimetres in height and up to 18 centimetres in diameter. It took the place of the cross and seems to be a relic of pagan times; and yet crosses, too, are found in these cemeteries. The *domovina* and *stolbets* bear witness to a certain religious dualism in the Russian mind, combining a physical cult of the dead with the more spiritual Christian teaching on the immortality of the soul. Sometimes there was also a small brass icon, which was inserted in the west side of the column, thus facing the *domovina*.

XV

XXI

XXII

XXIII

XXIV

XXV

XXVI

138 These icons were mass-produced in the eighteenth and nineteenth centuries at Vygovsk and distributed all over Russia. The whole column was usually decorated with carved designs. Photographs and drawings do more justice to these memorials than any words.

Modern cemeteries, of course, even in the remotest north, are just like cemeteries everywhere. The graves, surmounted by crosses or pyramids with little red stars, and adorned with photographs, are carefully maintained, surrounded by a little metal or wooden fence and planted with flowers. They somehow lack the sense of awe and mystery which haunts the ancient burial grounds set in the midst of the deserted White Sea dunes.

A village or *pogost* would have its own church, the centre of local life, standing out from and dominating its surroundings. Chapels were to be found in hamlets and, like memorial crosses, in places with a special spiritual significance, where a pious Christian might wish to make the sign of the cross. Most surviving chapels in the 135 north of the country consist of a basic log-built rectangle under a simple, gabled roof crowned with an onion dome. A *trapeznaya* (originally a refectory for the clergy and a parish meeting-hall) was attached to the west wall, often with a tent-roofed belfry above. Some chapels were little more than barns, while others were as majestic as churches. The main difference was that a church had an iconostasis but a chapel had neither iconostasis nor sanctuary, and its interior was modest and simple.

LAKE ONEGA AND KIZHI

It is very difficult to protect wooden buildings in situ from the ravages of fire, other elements and time. When, however, they are removed from their original setting, they lose their charm and vitality, and the cohesion of the remaining buildings is dissipated. Even restoration has its perils: if the requisite skills or resources are not available, great damage may unintentionally be done to the exhibits. One example is a chapel in the Onega village of Fedorovskaya, removed to the open-air museum of Maliye Korely. The village lost its organic unity; put more simply, it lost its heart. The chapel with its porch was badly restored. The pillars supporting the roof were incorrectly tapered, the carved designs on the *prichelini* over-simplified, the wooden roof-tiles laid flat rather than ornately layered. The columns holding up the belfry were incorrectly reconstructed. The chapel's gallery originally had a boarded balustrade but was replaced, quite inappropriately, with carved pillars. Half-logs replaced the flat-timbered treads of the staircase. In other words, a stylized mish-mash of 'antiquarian' detail took the place of scholarly restoration, killing the soul and destroying the context of this little rural masterpiece.

In general, museums make an excellent job of preserving the past, using details which have been protected and respected by earlier generations of restorers and craftsmen in the course of renovation. Two examples are the church of St Peter and St Paul on Lychny Island in Lake Onega and a chapel from the village of Avdotino, on the left bank of the River Onega. Both were drastically rebuilt in the nineteenth century when the porches were discarded, but carpenters managed to preserve the carved pillars supporting them, allowing modern restorers to calculate the porches' original dimensions.

141–42 *Trapeznaya* of the church at Petukhovo, Archangel Province. The attempt to deprive this wooden church of its wooden character illustrates the insensitivity of some 19th-century restorers to the quality and charm of folk art. Left: a column completely boxed in to make it resemble a masonry pier. Right: the removal of two panels has revealed part of the original carved wooden column hidden inside

143 Puchuga, on the Northern Dvina. SS Peter and Paul, 1788. The unspoilt narthex (*trapeznaya*) with wooden columns supporting the low ceiling, wall-bench and door leading to the nave

144 Fedorovskaya on the River Onega from the north-west

145 Avdotino. Original carved upright from the porch of the chapel, found hidden under the floorboards

146 Avdotino on the Onega. The chapel without its porch

147 Winter view of the Fedorovskaya chapel as now restored, standing in the Maliye Korely open-air museum, Archangel

XV   The church of St Lazarus, part of the Muromsky monastery, is the oldest wooden church surviving in Russia. Built at the end of the fourteenth century, it is a simple log rectangle, of a type common in Russia since the earliest days of Christianity. The monastery is situated on the south-east bank of Lake Onega, where a small river, the Muromka, flows into the lake. It was founded in the era of the Republic of Novgorod, by monks accompanying Novgorodian expeditions. Their mission was to establish the religious and political supremacy of the republic and one of their number, Lazarus (died 1391), is credited with the actual foundation of the monastery. According to sixteenth- and seventeenth-century chronicles it included two churches, a tent-roofed bell-tower and wooden cells, as well as various domestic buildings and the tiny wooden church of St Lazarus without the walls. The monastery was disbanded and later reconstituted; of its buildings none survived except St Lazarus, spared out of reverence for the saint's holy name. Apart from the western side-chapel, which was lost, it was preserved

149   by dint of constructing a new church around and above it.

We have no documents to indicate the date of the building of St Lazarus, although local legend insists that it was built during the monk's life, a belief supported by several archaic elements in its construction. To begin with, the logs

148   of the basic framework are grooved (for the reception of the next log) on the upper, rather than their lower side – a method obsolete by the beginning of the fifteenth century. Secondly, the entrance door: its lintel consists of two separate beams, joined independently to their respective jambs, inside and outside. The door-sill at ground-level is similarly constructed. (By the fifteenth century, lintels were made of solid beams, as typified in the doors and windows of a church built in 1486 in the village of Borodava, Vologda district, which was dismantled and later reassembled at a new site in the monastery of the Holy Saviour at Priludsk.) Thirdly, the sanctuary, beyond the iconostasis, lacks a ceiling. Fourthly, some legless tables – or shelves – crude and shapeless, are set into the corners of the church. Finally, the door is joined in the most primitive and rudimentary way to the side walls.

Other features of the construction of St Lazarus have much in common with

152   similar wooden churches. There is a low, 'dry stone' foundation of small boulders; the floor is made of massive boards, sixty centimetres wide, fastened with dowels. The flat ceiling is also made of boards, running from wall to wall and supported by a central beam. The *slegi* (purlins) of the roof are slotted into every log of the gable-ends, not into alternate ones, as in later buildings. Birch-bark is plaited with mast (the fine layer between the wood and the bark) to form wide sheets which are laid across these rafters. Some of the original axe-cut boards of the under-roof can still be seen, nailed to the *slegi*. The roof itself has been restored with sawn boards and only a few of the axe-cut timbers have survived. The lower ends of the

150, 152   roof-timbers are decorated with familiar motifs.

It is a tiny, modest church, ten paces long and three wide. You can touch the

150   ceiling with your hand. It is more like a barn or a hunter's shack than a house of God, but how tasteful, how fine, how delicate the relationship between man and building, how imbued with a spirituality more akin to art than to mere craftsmanship. It holds its own even compared with the magnificent cathedral of Kizhi, for the eye finds peace and tranquillity in the naïve grace and refined simplicity of its gentle silhouette.

148–49 The miniature church of the Raising of Lazarus within its 19th-century protective building at the Muromsky Monastery, Lake Onega. 148 – a corner showing its barn-like structure. 149 – its single cupola

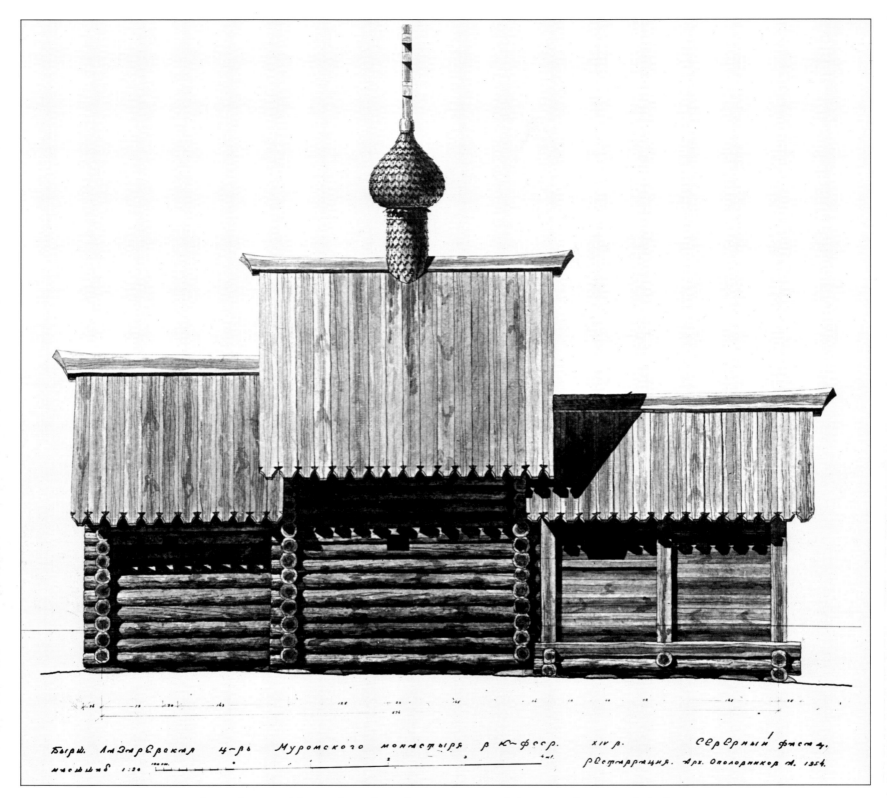

Быгш. Лазаревская ц-рь Муромского монастыря р К-фсср.   XIV р.   Северный фаса д.
масштаб 1:20   реставрация. Арх. Ополовников А. 1954.

150   St Lazarus. Northern elevation (the porch to the right was not part of the original structure). Scale in metres

151   (below) St Lazarus. Aboriginal detail from the sanctuary

152   St Lazarus, the oldest wooden church known to survive in Russia, under re-erection at Kizhi. It is seen here in something like its late 14th-century state, as the subsequent western porch had not yet been built on

The silhouette of a building, its proportions and its relationship to the surrounding landscape were important considerations to be taken into account when a new church was being planned. If possible it was placed on high, open ground, visible from afar, so that the wide expanses around it would form a carpet of white in winter, of blue and green in summer. Nature itself taught our early master-builders to perceive and appreciate the simplicity, clarity and strict proportionality of architectural forms, those very qualities we so admire in the monuments of traditional folk architecture.

XVI, XVII

Legend recounts that when Nestor, creator of the twenty-two-domed Cathedral of the Transfiguration at Kizhi, had finished his masterpiece, he flung his axe into the depths of Lake Onega, exclaiming: 'The world has never before seen, and never again will see, its like.' A beautiful story but there is some argument as to whom it refers. In his book *A Year in the North*, first published in 1890, S. V. Maximov tells a similar tale about the master-builder of the eighteen-domed Cathedral of the Resurrection in Kola (in the far north), erected during the reign of Peter the Great in 1684. Built of pine, it survived for 170 years. On the evening of 11 August 1854 it was set on fire after shelling by the English fleet blockading Kola. The English not only burnt down the cathedral and another wooden church, but also ninety-two civilian homes, as well as the wooden fortress (*see* Chapter III) and government depots full of grain, salt and wine. A mere six or seven buildings of this once mighty town survived the onslaught.

The cathedral was built when Kola was in its heyday. The story goes that the architect, or master-builder, was siezed by a fit of depression as he was about to place the cross on the central dome of the now finished cathedral. He sat on a hill overlooking his creation and wept from early morning until late into the night. His friends implored him to take some food and to rest, but he repulsed all their entreaties. Children mocked him and he did not drive them away. He passed several days and nights in the same way, gazing at the cathedral and weeping. On Saturday he attended vespers and returned to his solitary post. After the midday mass the following day he asked for wine and bread and salt. Townsmen and curious Lapplanders from faraway settlements gathered round the cathedral, waiting for him to make an appearance. Eventually he arrived, grim-faced but dry-eyed. After the service of dedication an elder passed among the crowd with the master's cap, soliciting contributions and the public was duly generous. Then the master climbed to the top of the cathedral, fixed the cross on the dome, stood on a parapet and bowed deeply. The crowd gasped and shouted: 'May God protect thee!' Then he descended and addressed the people as follows: 'Fellow Christians, come with me to our beloved river Tuloma, that I may speak with you.' At first the people were alarmed; but seeing his now calm, unclouded expression they were reassured and followed him. He stood on the steep river-bank, took his axe from his belt and hurled it into the swirling waters, exclaiming: 'The world has never seen, and never again will see a master such as I!' He threw himself into the crowd and ran to his house. After another day of fasting and sobbing he regained his composure but, despite the most fervent entreaties of his admirers, never took an axe in his hand again.

Legends must always be taken with a pinch of salt but these two stories may indicate that the same master was responsible for more than one cathedral in those parts: Kola, 1684; Kizhi, 1714, and possibly even Vytegra, 1708.

153 Aerial view of the Kizhi *pogost* in the midst of Lake Onega, seen from the south. The nearer church is dedicated to the Intercession, the cathedral beyond (then still under restoration) to the Transfiguration

153

154, 159

Let us now consider the Transfiguration in Kizhi, the sole survivor of all the multi-domed cathedrals built during the reign of Peter the Great. Its silhouette has a majestic and sculptural quality, especially during the endless northern summer days. We approach it from the village of Vasilyevo (the landing-stage of Kizhi), along the 'spine' of the little island. Lake Onega stretches away from us on every side. At first the cathedral's outline is misty, even ghostly. Gradually we are overwhelmed by its monumental clarity and grace, stark against the lilac-white sky.

It was built, reputedly from a design drawn up by Peter the Great, at a time when Russia was becoming a mighty empire. Not one single vulgar or superfluous detail detracts from its dignity, although in the late nineteenth century, incredibly enough, this unique masterpiece was 'restored' to the point of unrecognizability. Its silvery, shingled domes were wrapped in sheet metal and resembled shiny skulls. The living, flowing log walls were encased in dull boarding. This beautiful building was not destroyed, but perhaps even worse, was disfigured, mutilated, mocked. Churches began losing much of their original character as a direct result of the growing bureaucracy of the Russian Orthodox Church, which became a mere lackey of the autocracy. The clergy degenerated, as Lenin put it, into 'serf-owners in cassocks'.

The struggle to return the cathedral to its authentic beauty was a hard one, but eventually truth prevailed. In 1955, the sheet metal was removed and restoration of the shingled roof began. The island was without electricity and the restorers toiled ten to sixteen hours a day and into the evening by the light of paraffin lamps. Many designs were decided on the spot; the science of restoration was in its infancy and the heavy hand of bureaucracy was not yet an obstacle to the work. A team of carpenters, headed by the architect and restorer-in-chief (the author), was the final authority in case of dispute. By the end of the 1950s the Cathedral of the Transfiguration had re-emerged in its original splendour.

In the late eighteenth century a new, baroque iconostasis was installed, and this remained unaltered by the nineteenth- as well as by the twentieth-century restorers. Its virtuosity and richness of form impress even today. Its slender columns and cornices are densely covered with intricate carvings; the complex tracery of the 'royal gates' or 'holy doors' (the central doors of the iconostasis) is outstanding. The workmanship is faultless and yet the eye soon tires of the fanciful designs, harsh colouration and obtrusive gilding. True art is incompatible with the false gloss of vulgar ostentation and this iconostasis is quite alien to the rest of the cathedral. (For an older masterpiece of interior wooden craftsmanship, one should see the magnificent and intricate 'Holy Door', dated 1562, in the iconostasis of St John the Evangelist on the River Ishna near Rostov Veliky.) It is not elaborate carving and shiny gilt which capture the heart of the visitor, but the timeless simplicity and honesty of log walls. The massive door-jambs, the broad floor-timbers and above all the natural, unadorned texture of the shimmering, golden-hued wood itself leave an indelible impression on the mind.

The exterior plan of the Kizhi cathedral is quite simple, being based on a twenty-walled polygon. The central portion is an octagon, converted into a cross by means of four extensions, one on each alternate side. Two further, and progressively smaller octagons are superimposed on the central structure. Each extension has a stepped *bochka*, or barrelled gable, on two levels, each domed.

154 Kizhi. The Transfiguration, the bell tower and the Intercession seen from the south-west in the late 1940s. The churches are still sheathed in the ugly smooth boarding added in the 19th century and removed in the 1950s

155 Kizhi, Transfiguration. Central portion, with Holy Door, of the elaborately carved and gilded iconostasis, an example of Baroque exuberance somewhat out of keeping with the architecture

156 St John the Evangelist on the Ishna, Yaroslavl Province. The 'Royal' or Holy Door and its surround, dated 1562 – much earlier than the church in its present form (see 261). A magnificent work of woodcarving

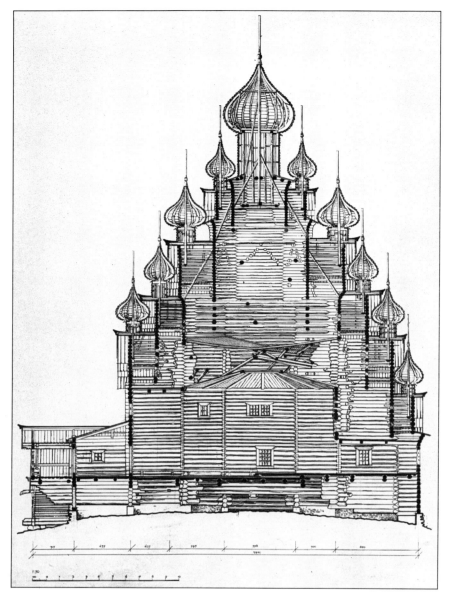

157 Kizhi, Cathedral of the Transfiguration (*Preobrazhenie*), 1714. This west-east section shows, among other structural features, the 'sky-ceiling' at the level of the lowest dome

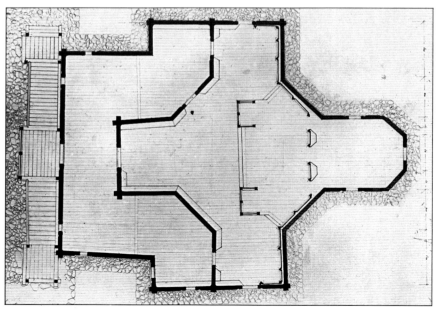

158 Kizhi, Transfiguration. Plan, with eastern end to the right. Left to right: *kryltso*; narthex or *trapeznaya* wrapping round the western side of the building; nave; sanctuary. The sanctuary is enlarged at the expense of the nave, owing to the unusual position of the iconostasis, shifted to the west. Scales for 157 and 158 in centimetres and metres

159   Shingles (*lemekh*) of stepped pattern from a dome of the same church

Above the extensions the eight facets of the largest octagon are topped by *bochki*, each with its dome. Higher still are four domes belonging to the middle octagon. A single dome, the largest, forms the apex of the smallest octagon and the whole building. The twenty-second dome, the lowest of all, is placed on the roof above the sanctuary.

The twenty-two domes are subordinated to a strict architectural design. It was an extraordinary talent that could unite all the various elements of the building into an organic whole, which no additions can enhance and from which nothing can properly be subtracted. The five tiers of the entire multi-domed composition are perfectly integrated into a single pyramidal form. The cathedral seems a unique monument created by a sculptor of genius from one piece of wood, rather than a building which must have been the work of many hands.

Now to the interior. The type of multi-faceted, tent-like ceiling above the octagon is known in the north as the 'sky'. Its framework consists of radial beams, slanting down from a central timber ring. Huge icons, lost for ever during the Second World War, originally filled the spaces between the beams. Plain boarding has temporarily replaced the icons, but the sixteen beams and the central ring are all original. Each is individually decorated with simple plant motifs in red, green, blue and yellow on a white background. The splendour of this interior contrasts strongly with the severe *trapeznaya* or narthex which seems to have been designed with the express purpose of soothing the vain and banal concerns of the congregation, preparing them, by means of image, music and atmosphere, for the solemn and spiritual exercise of their religious duties.

The location and construction of the cathedral symbolize a significant era in Russian history. Novgorodian documents imply that the Kizhi *pogost* was the centre of the whole trans-Onega area from the sixteenth century on. The 'Time of Troubles', which rocked Russia to its very foundations, did not spare this remote region: at the beginning of the seventeenth century foreign troops occupied all the Novogorodian territories, pillaging and laying waste the entire Onega region and the Kizhi *pogost* in particular. Polish military detachments, variously under the command of Governor Lisovsky and *Ataman* (chieftain) Balovin, Pan Gilievsky and Pan Pesotsky, penetrated Onega along forest tracks, lakes and rivers. The reign of False Dimitry brought tyranny, bloodshed and the tears of widows and orphans. In 1613 the Polish invaders massacred peasants who had taken refuge in the church of the Transfiguration, the modest, tent-roofed forerunner of the present cathedral, but three years later Muscovite forces, aided by the local population, expelled the enemy from Karelia. In 1617 the Stolbovsky peace treaty ceded western Karelia to the Swedes and Kizhi became a Russian frontier settlement. Powerful defensive walls with watch-towers at their corners were thrown up round the *pogost* and in 1649, by order of the Tsar, every male Onega peasant was conscripted into full-time military service while still being obliged to carry out his agricultural tasks. This was indeed a time when the bells of Kizhi called parishioners to resist the enemy as well as to worship the Lord.

The life of the peasants was hard. They were not serfs, although they paid a levy to the Tsar in Moscow, but the unending demands of military service, defence construction and taxation distracted them from their daily work on their smallholdings. In 1658, driven to despair, the 'peasant soldiers' petitioned Tsar Alexey Mikhailovich: '. . . our cottages, Sire, are empty, our wives and children

157

are dying of hunger, and our villages, Nikolsky, Shuisky, Spasky, Kizhi, Velikogubsky, Vygozersky and Kazaransky, spread out along the border, are defenceless in the face of enemy attack.'

Onega was the scene of many peasant rebellions. In 1648, Kizhi peasants had collected in the *trapeznaya* of the Church of the Intercession and violently attacked a judge, Fedor Maximov, one of their most brutal oppressors. In 1695, other inhabitants of Kizhi went on strike at the iron-works of a certain Butenant. 'They rang the bells of the church of the Transfiguration and people gathered from far and near, wooden staves in hand. . . .'

The year 1700 saw the beginning of the Northern War against Sweden for access to the Baltic Sea. It continued until 1721, and it was at the height of the war in 1714 that the cathedral was built. Russia was in the process of becoming a mighty sea-power. Many Swedish strongholds, such as Helsingfors, Abo and Vasa, fell to the Russians and local people could begin to resume a peaceful life. The construction of the magnificent Cathedral of the Transfiguration was associated in the public mind with Peter the Great himself and with the new era in the history of the Russian state.

XVIII As was customary in a northern *pogost*, a winter (that is, heated) church stood next to the cathedral: the Church of the Intercession is less majestic and more everyday than its neighbour. Built in 1764, fifty years after the cathedral, it betrays the first imperceptible signs of the decline in the tradition of architecture. There is a sort of dryness in its design, exemplified, for example, by the fact that each of its elements – entrance porch (*kryltso*), *trapeznaya*, nave, sanctuary – is of identical width, creating an oblong ground-plan with two corners cut at one end.

This is the commonest church design in the north, and is known as an 'octagon built on a rectangle with *trapeznaya*'. Older churches of this type had more varied dimensions. The *trapeznaya*, in particular, was often two, three or more times as large as the church itself, serving as it did the social needs of the local population. The church hierarchy bitterly opposed this social and democratic function and eventually succeeded in subordinating it to their ceremonial demands. These changes are easily discerned in the Church of the Intercession: the *trapeznaya*, though still a separate element of the building, is much smaller and less significant than the church itself. Nevertheless, as one of the finest examples of northern wooden architecture, it deserves its place next to the magnificent cathedral. It required faultless taste and creative daring to build the 'bouquet' of nine domes instead of the traditional tent-roof, thus successfully solving the problem of what to put next to the fantastic multi-domed Transfiguration. Should the new church compete with the cathedral or merely copy it? The architect found the ideal creative solution: the nine domes of the Intercession are a perfectly harmonious accompaniment – if in a minor key – to the powerful array of the twenty-two domes of the Transfiguration. The raised *kryltso* is deliberately and consciously placed facing the cathedral, its single short flight of stairs boldly asymmetrical in contrast with the symmetry of the church itself; this porch, together with the carved band round the octagon and the delicate cluster of domes, creates a feeling of natural, unforced spirituality.

In the 1870s the Church of the Intercession was horribly disfigured by external boarding, and the interior suffered even more grievously. The original multi-tiered iconostasis was replaced by a modern, eclectic and pretentious version.

160 Kizhi, Church of the Intercession (*Pokrov*), 1764. The boarded exterior as it was before restoration

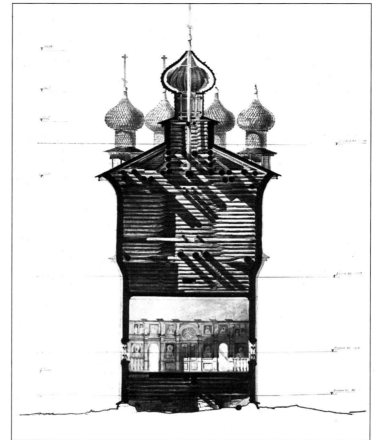

161–63 Kizhi, Intercession. 161 –
eastern elevation showing *bochka*
capped with dome above sanctuary.
162 – transverse section through
nave and octagon, facing east to the
iconostasis. 163 – longitudinal, west-
east section corresponding to 164.
Scales in metres

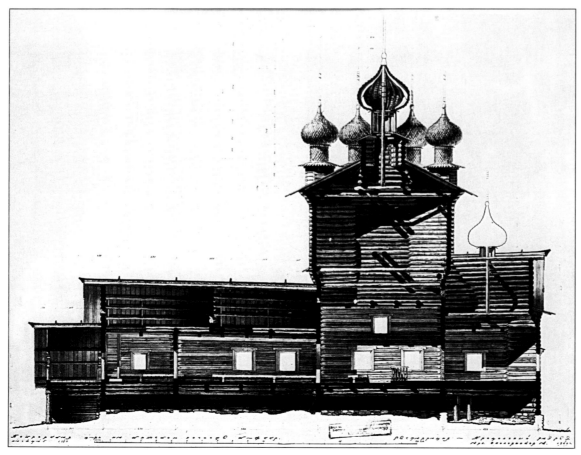

164 Kizhi, Intercession. South elevation as restored. Left to right: porch complex; narthex; nave surmounted by octagon on which the zigzag band has been reconstructed; sanctuary. Scale in metres

165 The same. Western view of the asymmetrical stair and porch complex or *kryltso*

XXI It was so out of place that the restorers in the 1950s were forced to dismantle it and recreate the original. Icons in the local northern tradition were selected from the superb collection in the Museum of Kizhi, which houses many marvellous XIX, XXII, XXIII examples of church art, fortunately preserved when the churches themselves fell into ruin. (The realm of northern icon painting is complex and diverse, and its study a source of great aesthetic enjoyment. Like northern wooden architecture, it is a folk art. The painters were peasants, artisans or monks from peasant families. No special studios provided training; professional skills and craftsmanship were passed from one generation to the next and from master to apprentice.)

The architectural ensemble of the Kizhi *pogost* would not be complete without XX its tent-roofed bell-tower, standing between church and cathedral. It was the last building to be erected, in 1874, when wooden architecture was already in decline, and it replaced a similar tower. The new version is of little interest, being a mere copy, but it has the merit of completing the traditional picture of the northern *pogost*.

A rich variety of perspective and foreshortening strikes our eye as we walk among the buildings of the *pogost* or sail round the island. The outlines of the churches and bell-tower merge or separate, creating elaborate silhouettes and fantastic new edifices. The finest view of the *pogost*, with its main entrance and welcoming church porches, may be gained from the western side of the lake, from which vantage-point all its various elements can be seen as parts of a subtle whole. The cathedral, for example, is more massive than the church, but a sense of balance is achieved by placing the church close to the bell-tower. The single flight of stairs making up the church porch is oriented towards the centre, creating yet another link between distant points of the entire set of buildings.

At one time a log fence surrounded bell-tower, church, cathedral and cemetery. Only its stone foundation survived, and another boundary, this time of boulders, replaced it. The present version was built in the 1950s when the rest of the *pogost* was restored. It is modelled on a typical ancient fence which miraculously survived in one of the remotest corners of Onega, the *pogost* of Elijah the Prophet (the popular St Ilya in Russia) in Vodlozero. It protects and defines the Kizhi *pogost* and certainly adds to its authenticity. Although the *pogost* was built by many hands over the course of more than 150 years it possesses a remarkable unity and leaves us with the feeling that it is the creation of a single mind.

Multi-domed churches were part of a very ancient Russian tradition (one of the oldest examples was the thirteen-domed cathedral of St Sophia in Great Novgorod, constructed of oak in the second half of the tenth century), but the Cathedral of the Transfiguration at Kizhi is now the only one of its kind. The Cathedral of the Intercession, in the nearby town of Vytegra, near the border with Karelia, was burnt down in 1963. Built in 1708, seven years before the Transfiguration, it possessed twenty-five domes, three more than its sister at Kizhi, for which it was the prototype. The design and building methods of the two cathedrals have much in common and suggest a single master. The basic design, a twenty-walled polygon, was very much favoured by the people of the north, as a story related in the chronicles illustrates. In 1490 Tikhon, bishop of Rostov, attempted to replace a traditional church, which had burnt down in the town of Veliky Ustyug, with a new cruciform church but the townsmen opposed it.

166 Kizhi, Intercession. Door from *kryltso* to *trapeznaya* (compare 163 and 171 below)

167   The surrounding log-wall or *ograda* of the Kizhi *pogost*. It is a recent reconstruction inspired by surviving examples at Vodlozero and Pochozero

168   One of the buttress-like projections on the inner side of the above

169   (overleaf) Vytegra, near the south-east shore of Lake Onega. Cathedral of the Intercession, 1708, in its 19th-century boarding.

170   (overleaf) Vytegra, south elevation as restored. Unlike the Transfiguration at Kizhi, the topmost domes here stood on a crossed *bochka* (*kreshchataya bochka*). Scale in metres

Быв. Покровская ц-рь 1708 г. на Вытегорском погосте Вологодск. обл.   Южный фасад.
масшт. 1:50 |‒‒‒‒‒‒‒| реставрация.   Арх. Ополовников А. 1956.

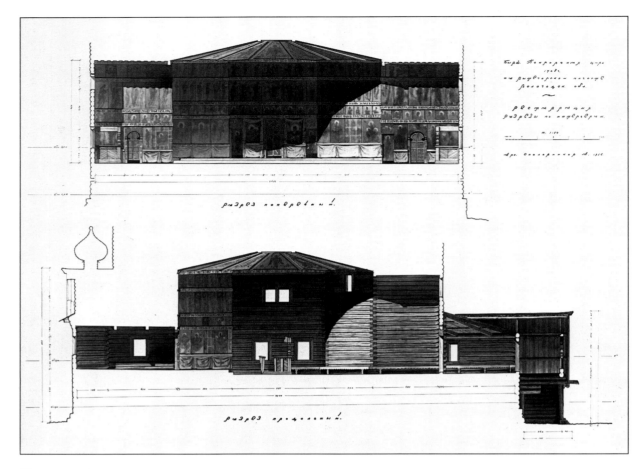

171 (above, left) Vytegra, sections through interior space with its 'sky-ceiling'. Above: north-south section facing iconostasis. Below: east-west section with *kryltso* to the right. Scale in metres

172 (left) Vytegra, west-east plan. Similar to that of the Transfiguration at Kizhi (see 158) but here there were three separate sanctuaries. Scale in metres

173 (above, right) Vytegra, decorative interior pillar

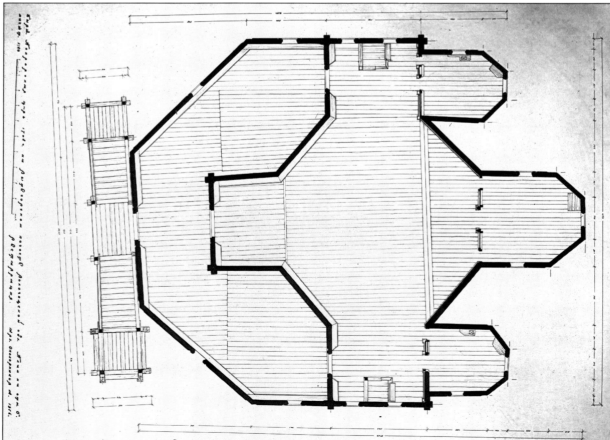

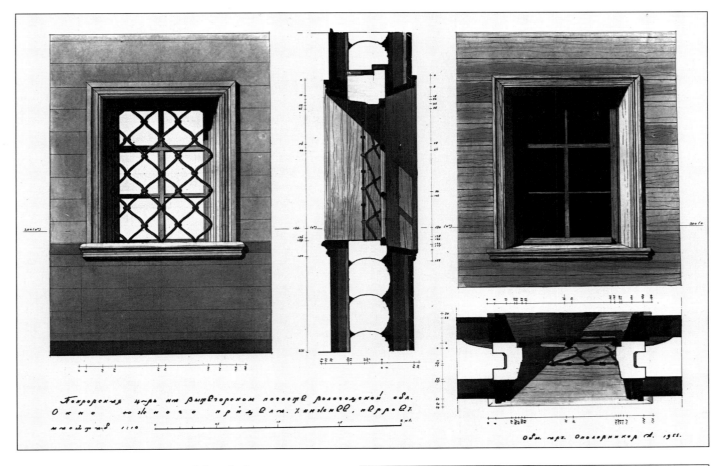

174–75 Vytegra, architectural details from reconstruction. 174 – sanctuary window from inside (left), in vertical section, from outside and in horizontal section. 175 – side view showing how each domed *bochka* overlapped the one below. Scales in metres

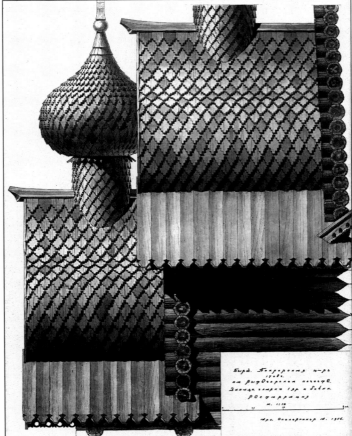

Eventually the people won the right to a round church with twenty walls – an octagon with extensions on alternate walls, as at Kizhi and Vytegra. (The same design was used for churches in the villages of Astafyevo, Seletskoe, and Nenoksa (pronounced 'Nyonoxa') in Archangel Province.

The design of both cathedrals is traditionally associated with the name of Peter the Great, and in the case of Vytegra it is even claimed that he sent a Dutch architect to supervise its construction; but this seems unlikely, as Russian craftsmen by then had immense experience in wooden church building and would hardly have needed the advice of a foreigner. Perhaps the 'Dutchman' is a myth intended to emphasize the very high technical standards achieved in the building of the cathedral, all the more since Peter himself had been apprenticed to a shipwright in Holland. There is, in fact, no trace of foreign influence in its design.

The Vytegra *pogost* was situated on the steep right bank of the river, eight kilometres from the town from which it took its name. It consisted of several villages, now known as the Ankhimovo settlement. In the past the settlement was dominated by the great cathedral, which was painstakingly restored in 1955, only to be destroyed by fire some eight years later. Two stone churches and a ruined bell-tower are all that survive of earlier times. Fortunately we possess detailed photographs, surveys and records of the cathedral, and these may one day contribute to its reconstruction.

There are major differences between the Transfiguration at Kizhi and the Intercession at Vytegra. To begin with, the latter consists of two, rather than three octagons, the third being replaced by a cruciform *bochka* crowned with a dome. Moreover, the Kizhi santuary is a single extension; Vytegra, by contrast, had three separate sanctuaries.

The Intercession was rebuilt several times and underwent its most drastic

169 changes in the 1880s. The local newspaper had reported in 1873 that a *kryltso* with two flights of stairs was dismantled and rebuilt without a dome. It seems that of the twenty-five original domes, four were removed from the octagon as well as the one from the porch. The reporter regretted that the interior, still unrestored, was not equal to the 'modernized' exterior – with its totally unsuitable boarding:

171 'The whole interior, apart from the recently renewed royal gates of the iconostasis, is dark, grey and primitive. In the middle of the church, opposite the south and north doors of the iconostasis, two large, crude platforms for the choir

172 obscure the icons. The windows are small, the walls unpapered, the atmosphere oppressive rather than numinous. We can but hope that change is on its way.' It is hard to believe that such poor judgment dictated contemporary taste, or that simple wallpaper was considered more attractive than the natural wood. Sure

173, 174 enough, the interior of the cathedral, so severe and majestic in its simplicity, inevitably suffered the brutal attentions of the architectural authorities of the day. A local patron of the arts, a prominent merchant named A. F. Loparev, donated funds towards the restoration. The massive logs were cased in boarding and decorated with colourful biblical scenes in the naturalistic manner of the period. An inscription placed on the west wall of the north nave in 1898 recorded the donor's generosity.

The first achievement of the 1955 restoration was to remove the boarding so

175 misguidedly added to the exterior and to put the four domes back in place on the

176 Kavgora chapel re-erected at Kizhi: only a chapel, despite the imposing belfry rising from its western end

upper octagon, thus recreating the original silhouette. The work was tragically and permanently interrupted by the fire of 1963.

Many chapels and small churches were scattered round the shores of Lake Onega and Kizhi Island. Some have now been transported to the open-air museum; others live on in their original surroundings, links in the so-called Kizhi chain. One of the most important chapels now in the museum is that of the Three Hierarchs (SS. John Chrysostom, Basil and Gregory, the fathers of the faith according to Russian Orthodoxy) from the village of Kavgora. It has the dimensions of a church and its graceful tent-roofed belfry dominated the whole village, symbolizing the spirit of local independence. In the museum, of course, it has lost its context and part of its charm. This chapel exemplifies the dilemma in which we find ourselves today, namely, whether to protect such monuments in museums, rendering them accessible to all, or to leave them in their original locations, in inaccessible villages, risking their complete collapse and permanent loss. To counter the inevitable disadvantages of museums we attempt to maintain some treasures in their original sites, as for example, the chapels in the villages of Vasilyevo, Korba, Volkostrov, Vorobyi, Ust–Yandoma, Podyelniki and many others.

XXVI

176–8

XXV, XXVII–XXIX
179–84

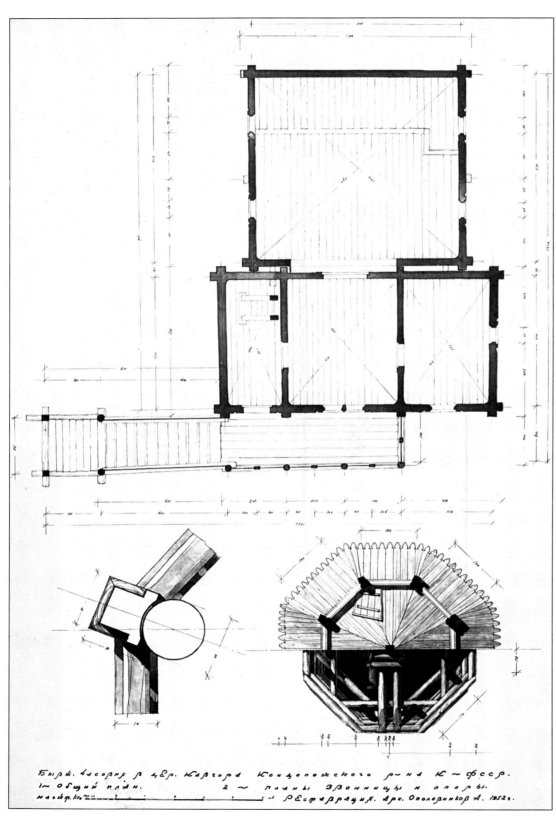

177 (left) Kavgora, architectural details. Above: overall plan, east side uppermost. Below: plan of belfry (half of which also shows the roof boarding); on left, one of the eight angles of the tower in detail, including a principal upright timber in section. Scales in metres

178 (above) Kavgora, the *kryltso*

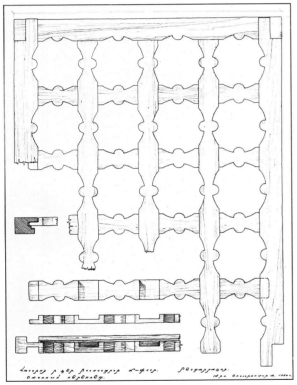

179–80 Volkostrov, chapel details.
179 – reconstruction drawing of a sash window grille. 180 – detail of a window on the south facade

Such chapels experienced two distinct building phases. In the seventeenth century they were simple log rectangles consisting of the chapel itself and a *trapeznaya* with a *kryltso*. In the following century the porches were dismantled and entrance halls with belfries put in their place. A new *kryltso* might be built on the west wall (as in Ust-Yandoma), the south wall (Korba) or on the north wall (Volkostrov). No two of these chapels are identical: dimensions and proportions vary significantly. The *trapeznaya* might be higher or lower than the chapel itself; the belfry might be a minor element or (as in Kavgora and Ust–Yandoma) come to dominate the chapel itself. The small dome might be placed directly on the ridge of the roof or onto a little octagon. *Kryltsa* were decorated in many different ways and the interiors varied, too: ceilings, for example, were either flat or in the form of a pyramid, like the 'sky' in the Cathedral of the Transfiguration at Kizhi.

The village of Yesino is a narrow strip of log houses along the north shore of Lake Onega. St Barbara's Chapel, dating from 1750, is set among old pines at the back of the village. This location is no accident: it goes back to pagan times when the local Karelian and Russian population were tree-worshippers and religious rites were celebrated in groves. N. Nikolsky wrote: 'It is worth noting that the tree itself was worshipped, rather than the spirit which inhabited it. The tree could cure by its touch, its bark possessed healing properties, its sap could turn into blood and its help and blessing were invoked with the incantation: "Holy tree, give us your help and protection. . . ." Bread, salt and eggs were offered to certain trees, which were adorned with colourful ribbons and garlands.' Thus Orthodox Christianity co-existed with the relics of paganism for many centuries.

Unlike other chapels of the Kizhi chain St Barbara was never rebuilt, although its exterior was boarded in the second half of the nineteenth century and its tiny onion dome dressed in sheet metal. It is surrounded by a low, boulder fence. The simple interior resembles most other chapels except in one detail: the entrance hall lacks a ceiling. Its shingled roof, however, is very typical.

The chapel in the village of Keftenitsy displays an original *kryltso* with a double flight of stairs and a carved tracery door. It is extremely rare and a delight to the eye.

181 Ust-Yandoma across the water from Kizhi, on the main peninsula of Lake Onega. The chapel before restoration

182 Ust-Yandoma's old graveyard by the lake

183   Chapel of the village of Kokkoyla, Karelia

184   Kokkoyla. Decorative motif crowning the chapel porch, whose gable also has *prichelini* and a *polotentse* suspended from their junction

185 St Barbara's chapel at Yesino, Lake Onega: an aboriginal, towerless type. South elevation. Scale in centimetres

186–88 Yesino, St Barbara: 186 – west elevation with its *kryltso* of the usual symmetrical type with two short flights of steps; 187 – transverse section looking east to a row of icons, substitute for a real iconostasis (scales in centimetres); 188 – the door from *kryltso* to *trapeznaya*

189

189　Kondopoga on the western shore of Lake Onega. The Church of the Assumption (strictly speaking the Dormition) of the Virgin Mary (*Uspenie*), dated 1774. A masterpiece of its type, which was never spoilt by external boarding (see plate XXX)

190　(opposite, above) Kondopoga. The church being too close to the water's edge for a normal *kryltso*, its two stairways were attached to the north and south walls

191　(opposite, below) Kondopoga. The *trapeznaya* with its two massive columns

KONDOPOGA

The industrial town of Kondopoga is situated on the north-west shore of Lake Onega, not far from Petrozavodsk, the capital of Karelia. On the outskirts of the town, well away from the multi-storey blocks of flats, we find the Church of the Assumption, a masterpiece of northern Russian tent-roof architecture, whose exterior had the good fortune not to be encased with boards in the nineteenth century. Its particular genius lies in the inspired use of a series of contrasts. The flowing perpendicular of the building is set against the endless horizon of lake and shore. The body of the church, a massive cube, broods over the delicate stairways of the *kryltso*. The tent-roof is a pyramid, reaching for the sky; the sober oblong of the *trapeznaya* hugs the ground. The log framework seems to grow from the earth; the fanciful decoration is unmistakably the work of man.

The design is the familiar one (also seen in St Nicholas of Lindozero, built in 1634) of a cube supporting an octagon, decorated with a carved band, and a *trapeznaya* in front. One interesting, though not untypical, feature is that the tall central octagon grows broader as it rises, giving an impression of extra solidity and significance. The heavy roof of the *trapeznaya* is gracefully supported by a pair of columns. The ornamental zigzags around the octagon are not purely decorative: their bars act as gutters, channelling water to small spouts in the lower angles. The carved *prichelini* fixed on the eaves of the western gable, where rain-water and melted snow collect, also had a practical function, that of increasing surface evaporation.

The church was built in 1774, at a troubled and dramatic moment in Russian history. Glorious victories over foreign enemies were combined with the pauperization of peasants, rebellion and rapid economic growth – this was the backdrop to the final flowering of Russian wooden architecture. Marvellous traditional tent-roof churches were also built in the north Russian villages of Konetsgorye (1752), Rostovskoye (1755), Nenoksa (1763), and Verkhnyaya Uftyuga (1784).

By the end of the eighteenth century the baroque and classical styles were strongly influencing public architecture; in Kondopoga and its surroundings the European influence of the architecture of St Petersburg was particularly strong. Cargo boats plied between Kondopoga and St Petersburg, carrying granite and marble for the palaces and cathedrals of the new capital. Builders and carpenters from the northern region followed the same route and eventually returned home, enriched by the new ideas they had absorbed in the great city. They introduced baroque decorative motifs into churches and peasant dwellings alike; this was the style that became firmly established and even dominant by the nineteenth century.

CHELMUZHI

The village of Chelmuzhi is one of the oldest Novgorodian settlements on the eastern shore of Lake Onega. This area is rich in ancient buildings, among them the Church of the Epiphany. It has graced the sandy shores of the lake, as striking as a lighthouse, for more than three hundred and fifty years.

197

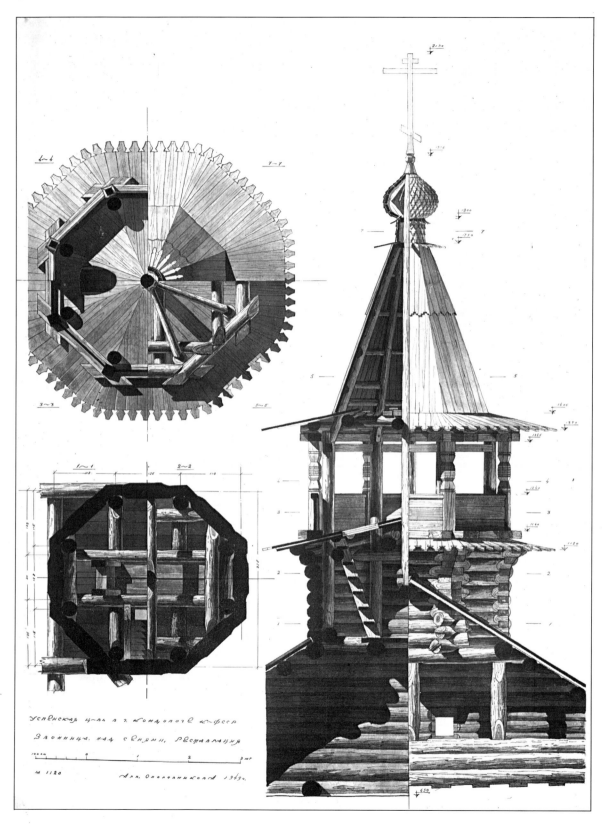

192   Kondopoga,
architectural details.
Right: the 'tent' tower
seen in combined
sectional and external
view. Left: plans at
upper and lower levels.
Scale in metres

193   Kondopoga. Detail of the zigzag band around the octagon

194   Lindozero, Karelia. St Nicholas of 1634. Another 'cube supporting an octagon', predecessor of the Assumption at Kondopoga

195　Verkhnyaya Uftyuga. Interior of the tent-roof, looking directly up, showing that the main structure of the 'tent' consists entirely of horizontal logs of steadily diminishing length

196　Verkhnyaya Uftyuga on the River Uftyuga, a tributary of the Northern Dvina. St Demetrius of Salonica. Here the basic plan is rectangular, the square base being converted to an octagon, which leads up to the tall tent-roof. The five-sided sanctuary is seen projecting to the east

197　Chelmuzhi, on the eastern side of Lake Onega, Karelia. Church of the Epiphany (*Bogoyavlenie*) after partial restoration in the 1950s

Its history is closely bound up with the turbulent events of Russia at the end of the sixteenth and the beginning of the seventeenth centuries, evoking the names of many prominent political leaders of the day. Princess K. I. Romanova (née Shestova), the mother of the founder of the Romanov dynasty, was imprisoned at the *pogost* of St Georgy, fifteen *versts* from Chelmuzhi, charged with sedition against the rule of Boris Godunov. She was obliged to take the veil under the name of Marfa, and the local priest, Yermolay Gerasimov, supported her warmly and unstintingly through all the years of her exile. Her son, Tsar Mikhail Fedorovich, rewarded Yermolay by presenting him with the whole estate, comprising Chelmuzhi, its *pogost* and inhabitants, and by freeing him and his descendants in perpetuity from all taxes, duties and obligations to the state. Marfa was pardoned by Vasily Shuisky in 1605 and fulfilled her vow to build a church of the Epiphany in the village in recognition of her miraculous salvation.

　　The church was probably one of the first to be built to the 'octagon on a cube with *trapeznaya*' design. There is a certain disparity between its two main elements: the octagon is placed not, as in later examples, at the centre of the cube, but above the eastern wall of the *trapeznaya*. As a result, half the octagon towers above the church itself and half above the *trapeznaya*. This odd feature is due to the fact that the church was actually founded in 1577, as a carved cross in the sanctuary testifies; it was then a simple log shell with a small onion dome. Marfa's contribution in 1605, recorded by another carved cross, was to rebuild and enlarge the existing church. It was rebuilt a second time in 1778, when the

197

trapeznaya was extended to include a spacious entrance hall with a tall, tent-roofed belfry. The next significant restoration was in 1844 under the architect Mileyev, who only compromised his integrity to the extent of agreeing to board the exterior. It would have been relatively easy to remove this abomination and return the church to its former glory, but in 1942 a misguided military planner insisted that both octagons be dismantled, arguing that they could be used as reference-points by German artillery. (The reasoning was odd indeed: by the same logic, the spire of the Admiralty in Leningrad, the bell-tower of Ivan the Great in the Kremlin, as well as many other monuments of our national heritage, should also have been dismantled but none were. The latest reconstruction of the Epiphany church was begun in 1953. The octagons were re-erected first, then the roof itself and the rest of the external boarding was removed.

The church with its two towers is very picturesque but its general composition somehow lacks balance, perhaps as a result of the disparity of the two vertical elements. The domed octagon is dramatic in its simplicity; the belfried tower seems fanciful and light-hearted by comparison. This mismatch is aggravated by some unsuitably ornate balustrades round the belfry. Another mistake was to rebuild the octagon two log-widths shorter than the original and without a *poval* (overhang).

The interior is traditional, with one interesting archaic detail: the sanctuary was separated from the rest of the church only by an iconostasis, rather than by a proper wall with an iconostasis set into it.

The iconostasis is conventional, consisting of three rows of icons. The lowest, so-called local row, displays the icons of saints specially associated with the area. The middle, or *deesis* row (from Greek, petition or prayer) contains icons of the Virgin, John the Baptist and various saints and angels who intercede with Christ on behalf of the worshipper. The top, double, row is reserved for the Old Testament prophets, with a representation of a church festival above each venerable head. The frames and settings are all original. The effect on the congregation is powerful and deliberate. We enter the church through the dark, low entrance hall. Passing through the roomier *trapeznaya*, we are overwhelmed by the church itself, a light, airy, candle-lit space vividly adorned by icons. (The iconostasis was removed to the Museum of Fine Arts in Petrozavodsk in 1963. Let us hope that one day it will be returned to its rightful home.)

ONEGA VILLAGE CHURCHES

Most churches known to us from the Lake Onega region were rebuilt and restored several times, and in the nineteenth century, as noted, many had their exteriors boarded. Some examples are St Barbara the Martyr (1650) in the now practically deserted village of Yandomozero; the Ascension in Tipinitsy (1756) and its contemporary Elijah the Prophet in Polya; and St Alexander Svirsky in Kosmozero (1769). Next to St Alexander, which was a winter church, stood the larger, summer Church of the Assumption. Built in 1720, it gained a bell-tower in the 1830s. Both churches, as well as the tower, were tent-roofed, creating an attractive and dynamic picture. A fire in 1942 spared only St Alexander.

COLOUR PLATE

XXVII Chapel of SS Peter and Paul at Volkostrov, seen from the south-east; in its present form 18th-century or later. The village stands on another small island north of Kizhi

XXVI

Several dynasties of local painters lived in the village of Kosmozero, notably the Abramov family. Until the Revolution they painted icons for local churches and in Soviet times, after 1922, they decorated sledges, shaft-bows of harnesses, window-frames, spinning-wheels, wooden crockery, cupboards and oven housings. The last member of the dynasty, I. M. Abramov, died after the Second World War.

XXXIII, 201–04   The churches of the Ascension and St Barbara the Martyr are within walking distance of each other. Although more than a hundred years separate them, their structural design and interior are very similar. Each had a bell-tower added at some stage, later connected by a gallery to a *trapeznaya* with adjoining *kryltso*. The Ascension is rendered more impressive by a high, raised foundation. Both churches retained their original small, square windows, although large windows were added later.

205   The village of Vazentsy, on the right bank of the Onega river, possesses the fine church of Elijah the Prophet. Like the Church of the Assumption in Varzuga (*see below*), it is cruciform, the cross consisting of the nave and four extensions. Round a cornice runs the inscription: 'In the year of our Lord 1786 this holy church was rebuilt. It is dedicated to the holy prophet Ilya and our Venerable Bishop, Alexander Oshevensky-Kargopolsky, in the reign of our most Pious and Sovereign Empress Katerina Alexeyevna' (Catherine the Great). This restoration, strictly according to the original design, demonstrates yet again the great devotion of Russian architects to the old building traditions, and in particular to the ancient cruciform plan. (Indeed, the design of the twenty-walled Transfiguration cathedral at Kizhi is itself basically cruciform, the only difference being that it is based on an octagon rather than a rectangle.) The sanctuary of the church has *bochki* on three sides, a common feature of many Onega churches.

KEM

207–09   The triple tent-roofed Cathedral of the Assumption (1711) in the town of Kem, near the White Sea, brings to mind Viktor Vasnetsov's famous painting *The Three Bogatyrs*, heroic defenders of the homeland in folklore. The cathedral too reflects the mood of Russian self-assertiveness and national dignity prevailing at the beginning of the eighteenth century.

The *kryltso* has two flights of stairs under a gently sloping roof supported by two carved columns. There is a roomy *trapeznaya*, similarly supported. The nave is a massive cube, bearing a lighter octagon which widens at the top to produce a rounded cornice. The roof is a high and steep 'tent' crowned by an onion dome

XXXIV   with a cross. A five-sided apse, housing a small sanctuary, is topped by a *bochka*. Two small chapels, miniature copies of the main church, extend the narthex to south and north. The varied, polygonal exterior of the church has a sculptural quality: further decoration would be quite superfluous.

Kem grew from a poor Karelian hamlet into a major trading centre in the seventeenth century. Among other interesting documents on local history in the town hall is a record in manuscript, begun in 1787 and continuing into the 1830s.

COLOUR PLATE

XXVIII   Gallery on the south side of the Volkostrov chapel. The carved columns supporting the roof are of characteristic north-Russian design

199

198   St Alexander Svirsky. The iconostasis

199   Inscription giving the date of this church: 4 October 1769

200   St Alexander Svirsky at Kosmozero, a village in the main peninsula of Lake Onega

201 Yandomozero, an almost deserted village among the minor lakes in the great peninsula of Lake Onega

202 Yandomozero, St Barbara before restoration. Originally 1650; westward extension and bell tower from the late 18th century

203 St Barbara restored, from the south. The fancy windows have been eliminated and boarding removed.

204   Tipinitsy, likewise in the main peninsula of Lake Onega, Karelia. Church of the Ascension (*Voznesenie*), 1756

205   Vazentsy, on the River Onega far to the north of Lake Onega. A constrasted, cruciform church type related to those in 211, 244, and 246

206   Polya, in the same area as Tipinitsy. Church of the Prophet Elijah (Ilya), 18th century. Both these churches are disfigured by external boarding

207   Kem, on the White Sea. Cathedral of the Assumption, 1714. Western elevation with central *kryltso*. At one time, as shown here, there were decorative *bochki* applied to alternate faces of the three octagons

208   Kem, Assumption, as it appears today after removal of the 19th-century boarding. The side-chapels share their main internal spaces with the central church but the three sanctuaries seen in this view are separate

209   Viktor Vasnetsov *The Three Bogatyrs* 1898. To the authors, the triple 'tents' of the Cathedral of Kem are an inescapable reminder of Vasnetsov's famous picture. The Bogatyrs are epic heroes of Russian folklore

It is entitled 'A history of the newly founded town of Kem, in the Olonets district, in the province of Petrozavodsk, built on the shores of the White Sea, in the Arctic Ocean, on the river Kem.' Dissenters fleeing from persecution founded a number of settlements and monasteries in the area following the *raskol* in the 1650s. After further persecution many of them moved into the town of Kem and by the middle of the nineteenth century it had become a stronghold of merchant Old Believers.

The very important Daniilovsky Monastery, on the river Vyg, was a stone's throw from the town. One of the characters described by Maximov in *One Year in the North* recounted: 'I heard tell of the recent persecution of the Old Believers in the Vyga area. I've always been the curious type, ever since I was a boy, always wanted to see things for myself. It was out of my way but I couldn't resist going up there to have a look at what was going on. . . .

'The church had been locked and sealed, the shutters closed and sealed too, with red sealing wax. Well, I thought to myself, you can pray at home if you want to. Shut the door, kneel down, God'll hear you, He's everywhere. Things could be worse. Then I saw the great bell-tower, and they'd taken the bells down. You know, it looked so wretched, that really upset me. . . . What did they have to do that for? The bells hadn't done anything wrong, had they?. . . The houses were locked and sealed, too, it felt like a cemetery.

'I had a look at the real cemetery. The crosses were all broken and scattered about. . . . It was a holy place, I'd known about it for years: thousands of people used to gather there to worship at the graves of Daniil Vikulich and the Denisov brothers, who founded the St Daniil monastery, and of their sister, Solomonida (she founded that convent on the river Leksa) and their old aunt. Lots of people from our village used to go and pray to them, too. . . . The fences were down, all pushed in . . . it broke my heart, I can tell you. The gates were locked and sealed, of course, and there were a few very old nuns sitting there. When they saw me they burst into tears. I whipped my horse and rode off, I couldn't help crying myself. That whole area was so rich and prosperous before all this happened, there were seven hundred nuns at the Leksa convent alone. The convent and the monastery respected the memory of Tsar Peter the Great. He forgave them and treated them well, just like all the Tsars after him. . . . And now, suddenly, for no particular reason, this dreadful attack!'

The spiritual devastation was as terrible as the physical destruction. From the 1830s onwards, hundreds of criminals were exiled to the area every year. Thieves, fraudsters, alcoholics and tramps were soon invading the villages, forcing the settlers to seek help and refuge from the rich, Old Believer merchant community of Kem.

VARZUGA

The remarkable Church of the Assumption (1674) still stands in Varzuga, a village on the Kola Peninsula far north of Kem. Varzuga lies on either side of the river of the same name, some thirty kilometres from the White Sea. From time immemorial this area has been famous for its river pearls, exceptionally large, round and even, and for its abundant salmon fisheries. At one time it was part of the Republic of Novgorod the Great.

XXIX

XXX

XXXIII

XXXIV

XXXVI

XXXV

XXXIX

XL

210, 211

The slender tent-roofed spire of the church, rising gracefully above three superimposed *bochki* and the galleries on three sides of the central cube, recall another famous monument of Russian architecture, the Church of the Ascension at Kolomenskoe (Moscow). The builders of the Assumption did not blindly copy the Kolomenskoe church but they do seem to have creatively reinterpreted it according to the canons of wooden architecture.

THE KARGOPOL AREA

Near the town of Kargopol at the source of the River Onega is the settlement or *sloboda* of Oshevenskoye. It lies on the right bank of a shallow river, the Churega. The *sloboda* actually consists of three villages: Pogost, Shiryaikha and Niz. Pogost is self-explanatory: there is an old cemetery with a wooden, tent-roofed Church of the Epiphany (1787) and a bell-tower. The church is attractively set among groves of birch and larch, although the effect is somewhat spoiled by the later exterior boarding.

In fact, most of the churches in this area are tent-roofed, but they do show great variety and liveliness. Another village which bears the name Pogost also boasts a most distinctive tent-roofed church, the Nativity. It stands near the road connecting Nyandoma and Kargopol, some ten kilometres from the latter. The facets of the 'pyramid' roof, though very steep, bulge slightly, and its apex is abruptly truncated. It bears an extremely thin neck, topped by a small onion dome. The exact year of the construction of the Nativity is unknown but it is mentioned in archives at the end of the seventeenth century, and many details of its design and building methods confirm such a date. The area is flat, agricultural lowland and the church is surrounded by fir and larch, and old moss-covered crosses and gravestones. The graves themselves lie under a carpet of pine-cones and needles. A nearby stone church is not uninteresting, but loses by comparison with its older, wooden companion. It is the wood itself which gives the Nativity an irresistible charm.

The lovely river Svidya flows between two lakes, Vozhe and Lach, where the Onega rises, and at one time this lake and river system was the waterway to the Belozersk district. The village of Astafyevo, on a bend of the river, was dominated by another tent-roofed church, which unfortunately was burnt down a few years ago. It was built in the middle of the seventeenth century and dedicated to St Nicholas the Miracle-worker. Its sanctuary had a *bochka* gable, supporting a small octagon crowned by a low and slender tent-roof. This design distinguished it from all other known northern examples, which typically feature just an onion dome on a slim neck above the *bochka* of the sanctuary.

The church of St John Chrysostom (1665) rises majestically above the flat fields near the village of Saunino, six kilometres from Kargopol. It stands in an old cemetery which was originally surrounded by a boulder fence. Its distinguishing feature is the asymmetric positioning of some of its elements relative to the east-west axis. Thus the roomy *trapeznaya* is 'displaced' to the south, with the result that its north and south facades are dissimilar. The northern wall of the *trapeznaya* is built in the same plane as the north wall of the church itself.

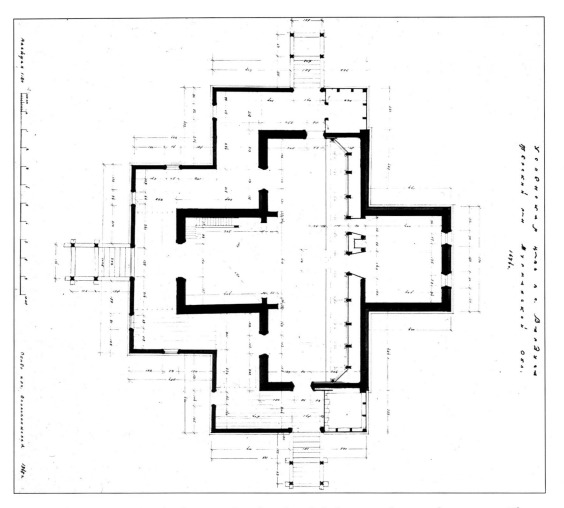

210   Varzuga. Plan, clearly showing that this church belongs to the cruciform group. The gallery encircles the north, west and south sides (compare 158 and 172).Scale in metres

211   Varzuga, in the Kola Peninsula near the northern coast of the White Sea. Church of the Assumption, 1674. A remarkable cruciform building apparently influenced by Muscovite brick architecture

212 Oshevenskoye, a village near Kargopol, which lies at the source of the River Onega. Church of St John the Evangelist

213 Astafyevo on the Svidya, south of Kargopol. The church of St Nicholas has been burnt down since the picture was taken. Its sanctuary was roofed with a large *bochka*, itself surmounted by a miniature 'tent' tower

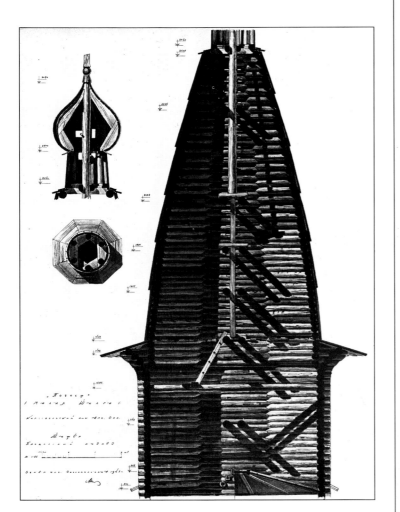

214–15   Village of Pogost, also near Kargopol,
Archangel Province. Church of the Nativity
(*Rozhdestvo*). 214 – vertical section of the tent-roof,
unusual for its somewhat bulging outline. 215 –
western elevation of the whole church, of typically
tall and narrow proportions. Scales in metres

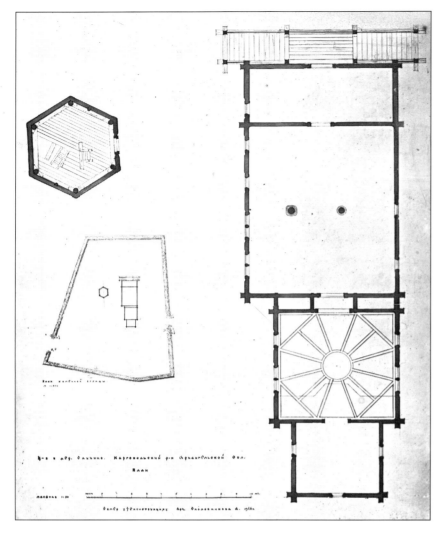

216 Saunino. Plans of the precinct and the bell tower to the
left and of the church itself (east end below). The church
plan shows an additional western lobby and a very large
trapeznaya which have a different axis from the rest of the
building. Scale in metres

217 Saunino. The bell tower with its unusual hexagonal
form and arched bell chamber

222

218–19 Saunino close to Kargopol. St John Chrysostom, 1665. 218 –
general view from the south with detached bell tower. The unsymmetrical
trapeznaya juts forward on this side and has its own small cupola. As
usual, the nave is crowned by a tall tent-tower, the sanctuary by a
bochka. 219 – a mighty wooden column in the *trapeznaya*

220 The Church of Our Lady of
Tikhvin in the village of Verkhovye on
the Mudyuga (a tributary of the Onega),
Archangel Province

Its southern wall juts out, thus creating a play of volume and space which enlivens the whole building, especially if one walks round it.

216, 217   The tent-roofed bell-tower, about ten metres to the south of the *trapeznaya*, is shorter than, and completely dominated by, the church itself. The tower is a hexagon, whose neatly dovetailed corner-jointing is somehow duller and dryer than the more ancient method, whereby the logs project beyond the point of intersection.

220   The traditional ensemble of sacred buildings on one site comprised two churches – one for winter, one for summer – and a bell-tower, but complete surviving examples are few and far between. One such group can still be seen in the village of Verkhovye on the river Mudyuga, a tributary of the Onega. It consists of the seventeenth-century tent-roofed Church of Our Lady of Tikhrin; and another church, built in 1865, with a five-domed *kub* roof. The bell-tower between them has been spoilt by various nineteenth-century attempts at restoration.

221 Lyavlya, near Archangel. Church of St Nicholas showing the ill-conceived restoration carried out in the 19th century

222 St Nicholas now returned to its original 16th-century state

From Lyavlya to Kondopoga

Tower-like tent-roofed churches, a variation of the watch-tower, are some of the oldest in Russia, and remind us of their military ancestry. One example stands on the steep east bank of the Northern Dvina River, in the village of Lyavlya, about thirty kilometres from Archangel. St Nicholas was built in 1584 by order of Anastasia, the elected governor of the Novgorodian republic, above the tomb of her brother Stephan. 'Between Kola and Kholmogor there are thirty-three churches of St Nicholas' went an old saying. At one time the cult of St Nicholas the Miracle-worker dominated the towns and villages of the White Sea coast as well as those of central Russia. Humble people worshipped him because he led a simple life devoted to helping others. He was the patron saint of travellers, seamen and merchants; his icon occupied the place of honour in every *izba*, so it is not surprising that St Nicholas of Lyavlya was especially revered by local people.

222

A monastery of the Assumption once stood in Lyavlya, an area rich in arable land and fisheries. In the seventeenth century it came under the sway of another monastery, the Antony Siisky; in the eighteenth it was dissolved and became a parish church. A new, stone Church of the Assumption, built on the site in 1804, has been so often rebuilt that it has lost any artistic interest. The wooden St Nicholas, dreadfully dilapidated, was closed for forty years and drastically rebuilt at the end of the nineteenth century. Thus it stood, mutilated and disfigured, until the 1970s when a scientific restoration was begun under the supervision of the architect V. A. Krokhin. The first phase involved the removal of internal and external boarding from the basic framework and the reconstruction of the original shingled roof. The original windows were also exposed.

221

The churches of Kondopoga and Lyavlya are at two extremes of a continuum of wooden tent-roofed structures. Kondopoga, some four hundred kilometres to the south-west of Lyavlya, boasts elegant proportions and graceful silhouettes but its Lyavlya forerunner, St Nicholas, with its powerful outline and brooding dimensions, epitomizes the grim beauty of inner strength and martial reserve. The most unusual features of St Nicholas are the dome and the drum supporting it. Domes and drums were made, with few exceptions, of several rows of flat, curved pieces in a vertical position. In St Nicholas, however, dome and drum were built of horizontal logs, exactly like the tent roofs of watch-towers. The originals are now on show inside the church and a modern reconstruction has taken its place on the roof.

Churches similar to St Nicholas were to be found in other northern villages, for example in Panilovo and Viisky Pogost (both 1600), Belaya Sluda (1642) and Vershini (1672). Their great octagons, built directly onto the ground, were as monumental as their massive tent-roofs were sombre. The decoration was spare and functional. No sign here of the flowing rhythms of later churches, but they were certainly superior to their plodding, barn-like precursors.

223–9

There is an old and wonderfully picturesque bell-tower on the outskirts of the village of Tsyvozero by the Northern Dvina (Archangel Province). It was built in 1658 and survives in its original form. Its construction features an octagon strengthened internally by nine upright timbers (one of them in the centre). The open bell-chamber reveals the carved tops of these uprights which support the roof. An even older bell-tower may be seen in the village of Kuliga Drakovanova.

230, 231

232

223–24   St Nicholas the Miracle Worker at Panilovo on the Northern Dvina, 1600 but lost about 1920. 223 – the typical symmetrical *kryltso*, incorporating two flights of stairs. 224 – Igor Grabar's drawing of the church

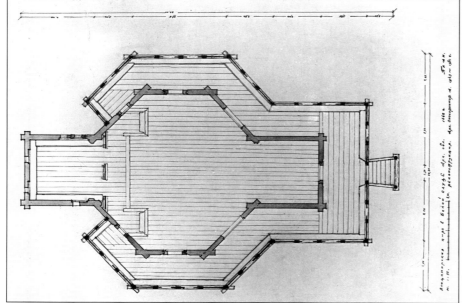

228

225 (left, above) Belaya Sluda, near Krasnoborsk on the Northern Dvina, 1642. The Church of Our Lady of Vladimir (a dedication which refers to the well-known icon).

226 (far left) Belaya Sluda. Our Lady of Vladimir. The original, east-west plan. Scale in metres

227 (left) Church of St George from Vershini (Archangel Province) now in the Maliye Korely open-air museum. This is another example of the basically octagonal plan

228 Belaya Sluda. Transverse section through nave and tent-tower, facing east towards the iconostatis. Scale in metres

229 Northern elevation of the same as it originally was, corresponding to the plan (226). Later the galleries were rebuilt and extended only to the north and south faces of the octagon. Scale in metres

230 Chukhcherma on the Northern Dvina near Archangel. The square-based belfry is (as shown by the flush corners) of late date: 1783. Behind, the 17th-century church of St Basil

231 Tsyvozero near Krasnoborsk on the Northern Dvina. The bell tower of 1658. It is octagonal right down to the ground, as the very earliest bell towers would have been

232 Kuliga Drakovanova on the opposite (left) bank of the river. A very early bell tower, though already provided with a square base

This is on the opposite bank of the Northern Dvina. It consists of a squat rectangle bearing a tall octagon. An open bell-chamber is surmounted by a traditional, high tent-roof. The very unusual way the onion dome sits, like a helmet, directly on the roof, indicates the great age of this tower.

233 Rakuly (Archangel Province). A bell tower based on uprights – very unusual in Russian wooden architecture – together with the two churches it served. Drawing by Igor Grabar

234 (below) Church of the Redeemer still standing on the site of Zashiversk, a long since abandoned settlement on the Indigirka River, north-eastern Siberia (see 124–25)

235 (opposite) Zashiversk. Eastern end of the church, its sanctuary crowned by a *bochka* with dome. The remarkable preservation of the church may result from rot being inhibited by the intense winter cold

SIBERIAN SACRED BUILDINGS

The relationship between central Russia and the far-flung regions has always been lively and mutually enriching in the field of culture and architecture. Teams of carpenters from the Onega, White Sea and Vologda regions frequently worked in Moscow and other parts of central Russia, while builders from Rostov the Great, Yaroslavl and Moscow brought their skills and experience to the northern outposts. Wherever they went and whatever they built, the results of their labours were formed by the ancient traditions of wooden architecture, deeply rooted in the national consciousness.

By some miracle, a beautiful seventeenth-century tent-roofed wooden church still stands by the remote Indigirka River, within the arctic depths of the north-eastern corner of Yakutia. It is the only surviving building of the old fortified town of Zashiversk, devastated in 1820 by a smallpox epidemic and never inhabited since that time. Even today the journey to Zashiversk is so arduous that only a helicopter can guarantee safe passage. There is no public river transport on the middle reaches of the Indigirka and cargo boats only ply there for the very short period the river is high. There is nowhere for aeroplanes to land and it is even impossible to get to the town on foot, as the treacherous banks are continually and dangerously eroded by the racing waters of the Indigirka. And yet resourceful men did succeed in braving these perils, and the lovely church is their mute witness. It is of familiar design, a rectangle bearing an octagon, crowned by a tent-roof with an onion dome. The *trapeznaya* is at the west end; the sanctuary is an eastern extension of the nave. There is no foundation, so the whole timber frame lies directly on the ground. The corner-jointing is of the older, projecting type. The roof is shingled and the log walls are hewn flat inside. The doors and windows are framed with solid jambs, the floors and ceilings are made of wide boards. In

236   A modest chapel at Stanchik in
Yakutia, north-eastern Siberia

other words, this Siberian church is very reminiscent of its contemporaries in the
north of European Russia.

In Siberia, as in European Russia, there is a great variety of wooden sacred
buildings. A tall, tent-roofed bell-tower, identical to the one in Tsyvozero, used to
dominate the single-storey dwellings of Turukhansk. Five-domed wooden
236   churches enlivened the fortified towns of Yakutsk and Ilimsk. Small chapels
stood, and still stand, in the arctic regions of Yakutia on the River Alazeya and the
lower reaches of the Indigirka. An old photograph taken at the beginning of the
century shows an ancient *kub*-roofed church in the village of Pokrovskoye on the
River Lena, some eighty kilometres from Yakutsk.

THE KUB ROOF

Roofs of *kub* form frequently displaced 'tents' in the eighteenth century and
became very popular, though not for long. Their appearance is a logical
consequence of the general tendency in Russian seventeenth-century taste
towards the picturesque, in sacred as well as in civilian architecture. An example
of the latter was the seventeenth-century wooden palace of Kolomenskoe, near
Moscow. The great dining-hall was covered by a vast *kub*. Such a roof was usually
supported on a rectangular base and adorned by one, five (most commonly) or
nine onion domes.

237 Permogorye (on the Northern Dvina, Archangel Province). Church of St George, 1665; weather-boarded in 1875

238 Permogorye, St George. The church has a curious type of roof consisting of crossed *bochki* surmounted by three, but not the expected five domes

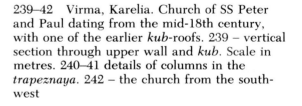

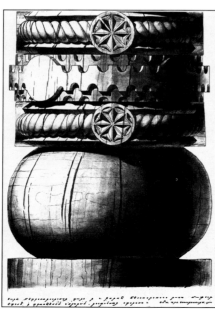

239–42 Virma, Karelia. Church of SS Peter and Paul dating from the mid-18th century, with one of the earlier *kub*-roofs. 239 – vertical section through upper wall and *kub*. Scale in metres. 240–41 details of columns in the *trapeznaya*. 242 – the church from the south-west

237, 238   In spite of the most vigorous attempts on the part of the church authorities in Moscow to impose the five-dome pattern on all Russian churches, their influence was limited to masonry buildings. Wooden churches modelled on brick architecture were actually designated in contemporary documents as 'stone-type' (*na kamennoye dyelo*). The very name indicates that they were concessions to bureaucracy, devoid of any original creativity. Craftsmen resented working on them because of their rigid predictability, which discouraged them from exercising their skill and imagination. Their constant search for new designs, which might gracefully complement the flowing and complex forms of onion domes, led them to replace pyramidal tent-roofs with the *kub*.

242   One of the oldest *kub*-roofs is to be seen on the church of St Peter and St Paul (mid-eighteenth century) in the village of Virma in the White Sea region of Karelia. Its main point of interest is the five-domed *kub* built over the rectangular nave. The elaborate lines of roof and domes go marvellously well with the *bochki* above the pentagonal sanctuary, emphasizing the majesty and solemnity of the House of God. St Peter and St Paul has an especially lyric character, set among the firs and mossy boulders of the endless White Sea plain, but what makes this particular church so crucial to the Russian heritage is the unique construction of

239   its *kub*. It is constructed of horizontal logs superimposed on an inner rectangle, six logs high, which in its turn is fastened into the external walls. Inside the rectangle are two intersecting transverse walls which give the *kub* its stability.

243   Elijah the Prophet in the Vodlozersko–Ilyinsky *pogost*, on an island in Lake Vodlozero in Karelia, is another example of a *kub*-roof church. Built in 1798, its principal architectural interest is in the sharp contrast between its two main elements: the long, low *trapeznaya* and the high, massive rectangular nave. The church's extreme symmetry is due to the rigid requirements of canon law prevailing at that time. A tent-roofed bell-tower, destroyed in 1905, stood in a strictly symmetrical relationship to the axis of the church. The entrance hall, *trapeznaya*, nave and sanctuary together make up a length of twenty-five metres – more than four times the width. The area of the church itself is larger than the *trapeznaya*: the unusually spacious sanctuary with two altars, dedicated to Elijah and the Assumption of the Virgin, is over thirty-five square metres. The relative proportions and the care with which they were distributed, together with the exaggerated elongation of the nave, are most uncharacteristic of old Russian wooden architecture. It must be said that this church, and others like it, suffer in comparison with older sacred buildings, which made imaginative use of asymmetry to enrich and enliven their overall composition. The roof is noteworthy for the unusual, though aesthetically uninteresting, positioning of its five domes. Only one crowns the *kub* itself; the other four are distributed at the corners of the supporting rectangle. A massive log fence still surrounds the Ilyinsky *pogost*, making an attractive polygon which corresponds with the contours of the shore and the surrounding countryside. The whole island *pogost*, set on a high promontory projecting far into the wide waters of the lake, is an excellent example of the subtle blending of architecture and the northern landscape.

244   The village of Turchasovo, on the Onega, has a bell-tower. Built in 1793 with a tent-roof, it also suffered at the hands of the restorers, ending up with a metal spire on a half-cupola covered with sheet metal. At one time Turchasovo consisted of a Novgorodian *ostrog*, on the steep right-hand bank, and a civilian

243　Vodlozero, Karelia. Church of the Prophet Elijah, with later boarding, surrounded by an ancient log-wall. The placing of four domes around but not upon the *kub*-roof is unusual

244

248–51

settlement on the left. Now its claim to fame lies in its two churches. The older (1768) is a nine-domed Cathedral of the Transfiguration. Five domes adorn the *kub* on the central rectangle; the rest crown the four extensions round the nave. Three have similar *bochki*, but the eastern (sanctuary) extension and its roof are tripartite.

The Church of the Annunciation (1795) stood next to the cathedral. It too was cruciform, but the cross was unusually stretched on its east-west axis. At the west end the uniquely spacious *trapeznaya* had a low ceiling of wide boards supported by six great, carved columns, instead of the more usual two or four. Although the two churches looked so different they seem to represent two aspects of a single concept. They were built to stand together and may have been the work of one master. The five-domed *kub* of the Transfiguration was reflected rather than repeated in the similarly shaped roofs above the side chapels of the Annunciation, and the elaborate lines of the *bochki* were echoed by the flowing rhythms of the *kub*-roofs. The superb complex of Turchasovo included all the finest elements of the multi-domed northern churches – tents, *kub*-roofs and *bochki*. The skills and experience of many generations combined here to produce the final perfect essence of seventeenth- and eighteenth-century wooden architecture.

244 The *pogost* of Turchasovo, here seen across the Onega River, made one of the most striking architectural compositions in northern Russia. Left to right: churches of the Annunciation (1795) and the Transfiguration (1781) with bell tower (1793)

245 A *bochka* applied to one of the eight high facets of the bell tower

246   Turchasovo. The *pogost* as it was. Right: the church of the Annunciation (*Blagoveshchenie*) burnt down after being struck by lightning in 1964. Surviving are the church of the Transfiguration (left) and the bell tower

247   *Kub*-roof with single dome belonging to a side-chapel of the Annunciation

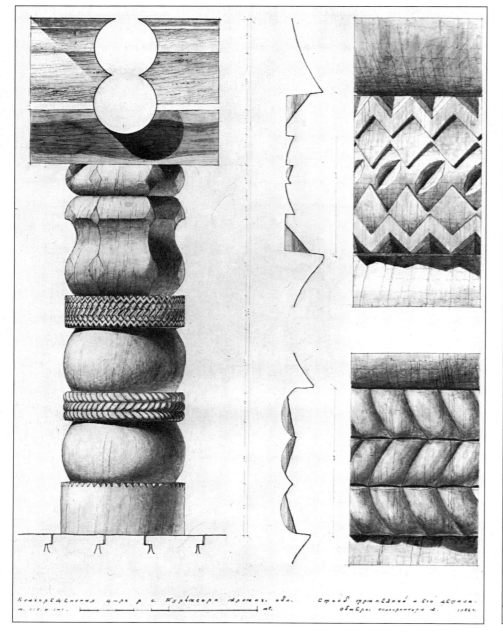

248–50 Turchasovo, Annunciation. 248 – a timber column in the *trapeznaya* with details of its embellishment. Scale in metres. 249 – the *trapeznaya* with two of its six columns. 250 – a squint (seen from either side, with detail of corner motif) enabling the iconostasis to be seen, and services to be followed, from the side of the *trapeznaya*. Visible in situ in 251. Scale in metres

251   The *trapeznaya* with view eastward to the nave and the iconostasis

CENTRAL RUSSIA

In northern Russia, away from the watchful eye of the hierarchy, churches continued to be built according to the traditions dear to the people. The situation was very different in central Russia, where wooden churches were built only in poor parishes unable to afford the costs involved in stone construction.

An open-air museum near Torzhok displays many interesting examples of wooden architecture collected in the central Russian district of Kalinin (formerly the province of Tver, together with parts of the regions of Novgorod, Pskov and Smolensk). One exhibit is the Church of the Holy Sign (*Znamenskaya*) from the village of Pylevo. Built in 1742, it has been carefully restored under the supervision of the architect A. I. Kustov. Its distinguishing feature is its narrow, northern side aisle running the whole length of the church. The aisle's pentagonal apse is level with the similar apse of the sanctuary, but separated from it by a wall. Outside, the two apses share a common timbered roof. The peak of the gable lies on the building's axis of symmetry, but the roof itself is asymmetrically divided into four pitches of varying size, resulting in a free-flowing silhouette on the eastern facade.

There are many more churches from the Novgorod and Vladimir districts displayed in other open-air museums near Novgorod, Suzdal, Kostroma and other places, but some are carefully preserved on their original sites. The most southerly is St Nicholas the Miracle-worker, still in the village of Vasilyevo, near Serpukhov, some ninety kilometres south of Moscow. It was considerably altered in the course of nineteenth-century restorations but it has now been returned to its original appearance. Built in 1690, it is of typical design, with *trapeznaya*, nave and sanctuary arranged in a simple row, one behind the other. Its only decorative feature is a gallery running round the building.

253

254, 255

XXXV–XLI

256–60

252 An abandoned and dilapidated chapel in Archangel Province, exhibiting the roof structure based on *slegi*

253 The two village churches (one wooden, one brick-built) at Pocha in the Province of Vologda

254–55   Torzhok open-air museum, Kalinin (formerly Tver)
Province. Church of the Resurrection (*Voskresenie*). A
noteworthy example of a tiered or storeyed church. 254 – its
modest porch adorned with *prichelini* and *polotentse*. 255 –
the five-storeyed, tower-like church viewed from the north-
west

256   Vasilyevo near Serpukhov. St Nicholas the Miracle Worker, 1689. One of the southernmost wooden churches of the 'north-Russian' style, about 90 kilometres south of Moscow. When this photograph was taken the surrounding gallery had been dismantled for restoration

257–60   Vasilyevo, St Nicholas.
Decorative beam-ends from the interior
of the *trapeznaya*

261   St John the Evangelist on the
Ishna, near Rostov Veliky, Yaroslavl
Province. Dated 1687, it is a storeyed
church of more modest pretensions than
Torzhok (255). For its splendid Holy
Door see 156

156, 261

The church of St John the Evangelist (1687; whose 'Holy Door' was mentioned before) is also still in its original setting, on the River Ishna. It is the only surviving example of old wooden architecture in the Yaroslavl district. Of the many legends concerning its origins, the most romantic relates that it came floating down the Ishna from Lake Nero, coming to land on the bank where the village was founded and named – Bogoslovskoye or St John the Evangelist – in its honour. Often restored and rebuilt in the nineteenth century, its original exterior is still encased in later boarding, but its proportions, design and many interior details have fortunately remained unaltered. The church itself is on the first floor, the ground floor being used for household purposes. A gallery, supported by massive log cantilevers, runs around the exterior. The rectangular nave supports a hexagon, which in turn bears an octagon crowned by an onion dome. The *trapeznaya* and the sanctuary, unusually for this type of tiered church, are surmounted by *bochki*.

Tiered or storeyed wooden churches first appeared in Russia at the end of the seventeenth century, although the earlier, tent-roofed churches were, in a sense, also built in several tiers – a ground-floor rectangle bore an octagon which supported the roof. The former developed, like the tent-roofs, from chapels of simple, rectangular plan. In some areas the tiered variety prevailed, in others tent-roofs were preferred, but from Murmansk to Yakutia, from Archangel to Kazan, they all shared one unifying factor: wood. It gives us the illusion that one single craftsman had wandered round Russia for centuries, building as and how he wished.

One commission to carpenters instructed them to 'build a church, guided by the old ways and your own sense of proportion and of beauty'. These qualities and the welcome symbolized by the carved entrance portal of the church of St John the Evangelist on the Ishna are the essence of the distinctive style which unites all the wooden buildings of Russia.

262   St John the Evangelist on the Ishna. The dignified five-sided entrance portal, with plan showing how the wall timbers are tongued to slot into the jambs. Below: enlarged rosettes

Select Bibliography

This selection includes sources of works quoted in the text and some more widely available studies, arranged chronologically by publication dates.

Onisim Mikhailov, *Ustav ratnykh, pushechnykh i drugykh del, kasayushikhsya do voennoi nauki* (1), St Petersburg, 1777

Pamyatniki Sibirskogo zodchestva (3), St Petersburg, 1830

Inok Zinovii, *Poslanie mnogoslovnoe*, Moscow, 1863

Prokhorov, *Ruskie drevnosti*, St Petersburg, 1871

L. V. Dal, 'Sokhranenie drevneruskykh pamyatnikov', *Zodchii*, 12, 1874

G. Peret-Tyatkovich, *Povolzhe v XVII i nachale XVIII vekov*, Odessa, 1882

V. V. Suslov, *Putevie zametki o severe Rosii i Norvegii*, St Petersburg, 1888

V. N. Malinin, *Starets Yeleazarova monastyrya Filofey i yego poslaniya*, Kiev, 1891

Olonetsky Sbornik, Petrozavodsk, 1894

V. E. Iokhelson, 'Ocherk zveropromyshlennosti i torgovli mekhami v Kolymskom okruge', *Trudy Yakutskoi ekspedititsii, snaryazhennoi na sredstva I. M. Sibiryakova* (3, 10, part 3), St Petersburg, 1898

I. Grabar, *Istoria ruskogo iskustva* (1), Moscow, 1910

M. Krasovsky, *Kurs istorii ruskoi arkhitektury. Derevyannoe zodchestvo*, Petrograd, 1916

N. Nikolsky, *Istoria ruskoi tserkvi*, Moscow, 1930

G. H. Hamilton *The Art and Architecture of Russia*, Pelican History of Art, Harmondsworth, 1954 (new edition 1983)

I. Grabar, *O Ruskoi arkhitekture*, Moscow, 1969

S. Yesenin, *Klyuchi Marii. Sobranie Sochinenii* (3), Moscow, 1970

I. Bartenev and B. Fyodorov, *North Russian Architecture* (translated from Russian), Moscow, 1972

D. S. Likhachev, *Razvitie ruskoi literatury X–XVII vekov. Epokhi i stili*, Leningrad, 1973

A. V. Opolovnikov, *Restavratsiya pamyatnikov narodnogo zodchestva*, Moscow, 1974

H. Faensen and others, *Early Russian Architecture* (translated from German), London, 1975

D. Buxton, 'Wooden churches of eastern Europe', *Architectural Review*, 157 (January 1975); reprinted in *Architectural Conservation in Europe* (ed. S. Cantacuzino), London, 1975

B. Fyodorov, *Architecture of the Russian North* (translated from Russian), Leningrad, 1976

D. Buxton, *The Wooden Churches of Eastern Europe: An Introductory Survey*, Cambridge, 1981

A. V. Opolovnikov and Ye. A. Opolovnikova, *Derevyannoe zodchestvo Yakutii*, Yakutsk, 1983

S. V. Maximov, *God na Severe*, Archangel, 1984

Glossary

Altar or **Altarniy prirub**   The sanctuary; the eastern extension of the church, rectangular or pentagonal. It is separated from the church itself by the iconostasis. Often mis-translated 'altar'.

Balyasnik   A traceried balustrade on balconies, galleries, belfries, etc., consisting of small, carved vertical columns supporting a handrail.

Bezgvosdevaya krysha   Literally, 'roof without nails'; a roof constructed by placing sloping flat boards across horizontal timbers (*slegi*, q.v.) running along the length of the roof, as opposed to the widespread method using sloping rafters. The boards are supported at their base by a hollowed-out log (*potok*, q.v.), held by *kuritsi* (q.v.). Built without a single nail, such a roof is very durable.

Boinitsa   Small loophole or embrasure, usually wider on the inside, for firing hand-held weapons.

Bochka   A decorative form of gable much used in wooden churches. In end view (or in section) it has the shape of an ogee arch (or of an onion dome seen in silhouette), culminating in a sharp point. *Kreshchataya bochka* is a combination of two intersecting *bochki*, sometimes used in churches.

Brus   (1) a log, roughly trimmed on two sides only. (2) a type of house, all of whose constituents are built in an oblong under one sloping roof.

Chasha   A large groove cut across one log, in such a way that another log can interlock with it.

Chelnok   See *oblas*.

Chernaya krovlya   An internal gabled roof, usually placed above a *nebo* ceiling (q.v.) in winter churches.

Chernososhnie krestyane   Russian peasants (from the fourteenth to the seventeenth century) living on state land. When this land was given over to landowners, these peasants became private serfs. By the end of the seventeenth century they were to be found only in northern Russia and Siberia. At the beginning of the eighteenth century they were redesignated as state peasants.

Chesnok   A continuous line of fencing, consisting of stakes slanting towards each other, serving as an obstacle to attackers.

Chetverik   A square building or section of a building.

Contreforce (from French *contrefort*)   A buttress or counterforce. Massive log giving additional support to a wall and counteracting its outward thrust.

Dvatsatistenok   A cruciform, twenty-walled structure consisting of an octagon and four rectangular extensions, placed symmetrically, adjoining the octagon.

Dymnik   (1) an exterior smokestack for chimneyless dwellings. (2) a chimney.

Fronton (from French)   A pediment; triangular part of a log wall, a pitched gable.

Frontonniy poyas   A decorative zig-zag belt round an octagon which has the function of protecting the lower walls from rain-damage.

Galerea   A long balcony supported by columns or extended log-ends.

Gat   A pathway made of logs over a swamp or bog.

Glagol   A type of house built in the shape of a Russian capital 'G' (or inverted Roman capital 'L'), i.e., the working quarters are placed at a right angle to the living quarters.

Glava   An onion dome with a cross above, crowning the whole building or one part of it.

Gont   Short roof boards used together with shingles (wooden roof tiles) for the curvilinear surfaces of *bochki*, tent-roofs and *kub*-roofs, etc.

Gornitsa   The best room in the peasant's house, on the principal floor (from *gorniy*, meaning 'upper').

Gorodnya   A section of a fortified log wall, packed with stones or earth.

Gulbishche   A balcony surrounding a building on two or three sides.

Ikonostas (English: iconostasis, from Greek)   The strictly canonical arrangement of icons, almost invariably placed in several rows, forming a screen between the sanctuary and the nave of the church. In chapels (which usually have no sanctuary) the *ikonostas* is placed directly on the east wall.

Izba   A peasant house or hut, constructed of interlocking logs. In a narrower sense, the living-room(s) of such a house.

Kamenka or **kamelek**   A crude hearth made of stones (not bound together by mortar, etc.). Smoke drifts through the open door, or is extracted through a hole specially cut into the wall.

Kamnemet   A fourteenth-century siege-engine, used to catapult pieces of brick, iron, stone and cannon-balls over fortress walls.

Khoromi   The complex of living and working quarters connected by one or more internal passages.

Khryash   A mixture of stone, rubble and earth, used for packing *gorodnya* (q.v.) and *tarassa* (q.v.).

Klet   Literally, 'cage'. A covered rectangular log framework as in domestic buildings and simpler churches; compare *srub*.

Kliros   The area of a church reserved for the choir.

Koch   The general name for many different kinds of boat, used by Russians to explore the Arctic Ocean in the sixteenth and seventeenth centuries.

Kokora   The hook of a *kuritsa* (q.v.).

Kokoshnik   A decorative architectural feature, a miniature version of the *bochka* (q.v.). *Kokoshniki* were placed on the walls and round the necks of the central onion domes, mostly in brick-built churches.

Konek   The crown or ridge of a roof.

Konevaya slega   The topmost (ridge) beam of a roof constructed without nails. See *slegi*.

Koshchatoe or **krasnoe okno**   Literally, 'beautiful window'. A window framed by smoothed or planed surrounds.

Koster   A pyramidal log structure.

Kreml   The central part of an ancient town, surrounded by fortress walls. *Kremlin*.

Krepost   A fortress.

Kruzhala or **zhuravtsi**   A frame for onion domes and *bochki* (*bochka*, q.v.), consisting of vertical boards nailed or dowelled together.

Kryltso   The whole complex of a porch with its associated roofed stairway(s). Compare *papert*.

Kub   A tetrahedral roof on a rectangular base. Its shape recalls a massive onion dome, or *bochka* (q.v.), but it replaces the whole of a normal roof and may be surmounted by a dome or domes.

Kuritsa   An element in roofs constructed without nails (*bezgvosdevaya krysha*, q.v.), i.e., a tree-trunk with one of its roots left as a hook (*kokora*), used to support the *potok* (q.v.).

Kurnaya izba   A peasant house or hut without a chimney. Smoke from the hearth drifts directly into the room and is extracted through the door, windows, or *dymnik* (q.v.) on the roof.

Labaz   Storehouse or barn.

Lapa (*v lapu*)   An arrangement of interlocking logs in a wall, in which the ends of the logs do not project beyond the point of intersection. Compare *oblo*.

Lemekh   Shingles, wooden tiles.

Lukovitsa   Onion dome.

Makovka   Dome of a church or chapel.

Matitsa   The main horizontal beam supporting a timber ceiling.

Mashikuli (from French *mâchicoulis*) An upper range of embrasures or loopholes.

Mitropolit (English: Metropolitan) One of the highest officials of the church, bishop of a 'metropolis', i.e., a capital city or province in the Graeco-Roman empire. Before the introduction of the Patriarchate in 1589, the *mitropolit* stood at the head of the Russian Orthodox Church.

Most Bridge. In another technical sense, floor.

Nadolbi A fence of sharpened stakes presenting a formidable obstacle to attackers.

Nagel (German 'nail') or **shpon** Wooden nail or dowel.

Nagorodnya A low turret with embrasures, built on top of a watch-tower.

Nakat A layer of beams and logs making up the ceiling of a log building.

Nalichnik Window-frame, often elaborately carved. *Nalichniki* incorporate shutters, as a rule no longer functional.

Nebo Literally, 'sky' or 'heaven'. A type of ceiling, often found in wooden churches in northern Russia. At its centre is a huge circle, with a number of beams radiating out from it to the walls. The space between the beams is decorated with icons, as is the inner circle itself.

Neitralnie nasloyenia Extraneous features of a building, added later, which although anachronistic, may be of independent artistic value. For example, baroque iconostases substituted in the eighteenth century for ancient originals.

Oblam or **brustver** Attic rooms on the upper part of a fortress wall or tower, sometimes extending round the whole perimeter.

Oblas or **chelnok** A dug-out canoe.

Oblo (*v oblo*) An arrangement of interlocking logs in a wall, where the ends of the logs project beyond the point of intersection. Compare *lapa*.

Obreshetka A general term for many kinds of roof-frame.

Obrub A supporting wall, made of logs, built to strengthen earthworks. It consists of slanting logs held together by horizontal struts.

Ochep A strong, flexible pole, fixed between the ceiling and ceiling-joist, for suspending a child's cradle.

Okhlyupen *Shelom* (q.v.).

Okolitsa The outskirts of a village; or the gate in the fence surrounding a village.

Optimalniy oblik pamyatnika The harmonious synthesis of the original constituents of an ancient and historic architectural ensemble, with authentically restored elements and later additions which, though not in keeping with the original style, are nevertheless of independent artistic value.

Oseki A simple fence of slanting stakes.

Ostatki Log-ends projecting at the corners.

Ostrog A fortified settlement protected by a wooden wall.

Ovin A shed for storing hay.

Papert A gallery (usually open) surrounding three sides of a church.

Pererub A partition or internal wall in a log framework.

Pishal A type of arquebus or blunderbuss used in Russia from the fifteenth to the seventeenth century.

Piyatina The term for the five territorial units of the Republic of Novgorod the Great (Vodskaya, Obonezhskaya, Derevskaya, Bezhedskaya and Shelonskaya).

Plakha or **plastina** One half of a log, split (later sawn) lengthwise, used for floors and ceilings. In ancient times, massive logs were hollowed and used as coffins.

Pochinok *Vystavki, vyselki* (q.v.).

Podklet The ground floor (or space below the main floor) of a wooden building. In churches, generally used for secular purposes.

Podtesok The lower layer of roof-timbers (*tes*, q.v.).

Podzor A carved board placed on the lower edge of a roof, porch, bench, etc.

Pogost The term originally applied to the administrative centre of an area, and to the area itself. Later, a cemetery with its church and associated clerical dwellings, or simply a fenced cemetery.

Politsa The lower, gently sloping and overhanging part of a tent-roof or gabled roof. It serves to throw rain or snow clear of the walls below.

Polotentse A short, carved board hanging from the apex of a gable and covering the point of junction of *prichelini* (q.v.). Also used for the lower, projecting ends of the *prichelini* themselves.

Pomochi *Vypuski* (q.v.).

Portal An arched portal of a church. Compare *kryltso*.

Posad An urban (trading) quarter.

Potainoy zub or **potai** A small rectangular lug in a log, set in a specially cut groove, whose purpose is to strengthen the corner-joints of projecting, interlocking logs.

Potok Part of a roof without nails (*bezgvosdevaya krysha*, q.v.). It is a grooved log, running the length of the eave, supporting the roof-boards, whose lower ends fit into the groove. In its turn, the *potok* is supported by *kuritsi* (q.v.).

Poval The widened, somewhat cornice-like top layers of a log wall, especially common at the base of tent-roofs and commonly overhung by the *politsa* (q.v.).

Povalusha A living-room built over a Russian *izba* (q.v.), used as a bedroom in the summer.

Povet The first floor of the working quarters of the *izba* (q.v.).

Povolniki *Ushkuiniki* (q.v.).

Prichelina The board attached to the eaves, especially at the gable end of roofs, and covering the ends of the *slegi* (q.v.). These *prichelini* are usually treated decoratively, being elaborately carved. Approximate English equivalent: bargeboards.

Pridel A side-altar or side-chapel.

Prikaz A government department in Muscovy. Also an order or command.

Prirub An extension (of secondary importance) to a log building, often lower than the main building.

Priyaslo (1) part of the fortress wall between two towers. (2) type of fence constructed of horizontal stakes.

Protopop An archaic title, not used since the beginning of the nineteenth century, for the archpriest of the Russian Orthodox Church.

Samtsovaya krysha A roof constructed without nails (*bezgvosdovaya krysha*, q.v.).

Sazhen An old Russian unit of length. One *sazhen* = 2.13 metres.

Seni A room located immediately behind the entrance porch; an entrance hall.

Shater (pronounced *shatyor*) Literally, 'tent'. Low tent-roofs on a square base (as in many defensive towers); can be described as 'pyramidal'. The term tent-roof is here retained for the relatively tall, sometimes spire-like octagonal roofs of churches and belfries.

Shea Literally, 'neck'. The drum bearing a dome on the roof of a church.

Shelom or **okhlyupen** A hollowed log forming the ridge of the roof.

Shestok The area in front of the hearth of a Russian oven.

Shkant A pin or lug holding two wooden constructions together.

Shponka A dowel. Compare *nagel*.

Shtraby Grooved, flattened sections along or across log walls, to enable structural additions to be more easily attached.

Skit A term used to describe a remote Old Believers' settlement, a refuge both from serfdom and persecution by the official church. Hermitage.

Slegi Horizontal timbers supporting *kuritsi* (q.v.). They are the principal support of the roof. Approximate English equivalent: purlins.

Sloboda: a settlement exempt from state duties and taxes.

Slukhi Small holes, set in the floors and ceilings of multi-storey watch-towers, through which orders and information could be communicated.

Soleya The raised floor in front of a church sanctuary.

Soroka or **stamik** A wooden bushing-key or dowel holding together the *konevaya slega* and *shelom* (q.v.).

Srub The basic log framework of any wooden building.

Stolb The tall, vertical element of a building, including watch-towers and churches. In the case of a church it would normally surmount the nave.

Strug A flat-bottomed rowing-boat used for transporting goods by river.

Susek A bin for storing flour or grain in a granary.

Sves A projection from the upper part of a building.

Syeszhaya izba The administrative building within a *pogost* (q.v.) or

fortress. It contained archives, offices and a prison.

Tarassa A *continuous* double log wall, the space between being packed with stones, rubble or earth (compare *gorodnya*).

Tes Roof boarding.

Tetiva or **kosour** A beam supporting a flight of stairs.

Traditsionie nasloyeniya Relatively late elements of a building, executed according to the traditions of folk architecture. For example, the authentic restoration of a roof.

Trapeznaya or **predkhramie** The western extension of a church (originally a separate building for public meetings and a waiting-hall for the congregation, etc.). Later the *trapeznaya* itself could be used for church services. Equivalent of narthex.

Tyablo (1) horizontal beams, shelves, on which icons are placed in an *ikonostas* (q.v.). (2) sloping beams in the pyramidal ceiling of a church (*nebo*, q.v.).

Tyn or **tynovaya stena** A fortress wall made of vertical, sharpened logs.

Ushkuiniki or **povolniki** Members of Novgorodian pioneering detachments. They travelled by boat (*ushkui*) along the northern rivers, seeking trading contacts and colonizing the new territories.

Venets One row of horizontal timbers, interlocking at the corners.

Vereiya A column by the gates.

Verkh The upper part of the *stolb* (q.v.) which determined the architectural composition and design of the church.

Verst Old Russian unit of distance equivalent to two-thirds of a mile or 1.067 km.

Veshala (1) long thin tree-trunks, with some branches not removed (though cut short), for hanging and drying hay. (2) two vertical poles and a cross-piece for the same purpose.

Vezha The watch-tower of a fortress.

Volokovoe okno A tiny window (without glass), opened and shut by means of a sliding board.

Volyuta Volute. Introduced into wooden architectural carving from stone and often used in *nalichniki* (q.v.).

Vorobina The upper, moving part of a windmill.

Vorontsi Long wooden shelves running along the walls of an *izba* (q.v.).

Vorotnik or **yepancha** (*yepancheviy vorotnik*) Decorative work at the base of an onion dome and on the drum supporting the dome. It consists of wooden tiles, similar to shingles.

Vosmerik Octagon; any octagonal part of a building.

Vsvos A ramp (for carts, etc.) leading to the first floor of the working quarters of an *izba* (q.v.).

Vypuski or **pomochi** Consoles or cantilevers, consisting of extended ends of beams projecting from the log shell, which support eaves of roofs, external stairways, etc.

Vystavki (*vyselki* or *pochinki*) Hamlets consisting of a few houses. They sprang up as peasants moved out of bigger villages in search of more fertile land.

Yarus A tier. *Yarusne tserkvy*: churches whose roofs rise in several tiers or storeys.

Yasak A tax levied from the sixteenth to the eighteenth century on the native population of the Volga and Siberia. Originally it was paid in furs; from the end of the seventeenth century in cash.

Yazitsi Peoples, nations, especially as differentiated by language.

Yepancha *Vorotnik* (q.v.).

Zankovaya kaltso The wooden circle at the centre of a pyramidal ceiling (*nebo*, q.v.), from which radiate a number of slanting beams.

Zaplot A solid fence made of horizontal logs.

Zaseka Extended defence lines, consisting of partly felled trees, earthworks and ditches, and sometimes incorporating stretches of lake or river.

Zatyn The area beyond the fortress wall (*tyn*), either a small earthwork or elevated log rampart (used as a shooting platform).

Zhuravtsi *Kruzhala* (q.v.).

Zimove (1) a simple Russian winter settlement in Siberia. (2) a hunter's cabin.

Zvonitsa Belfry or bell-tower.

Index